BETTER IN 52 WEEKS

ACTION STEPS TO A BETTER BUSINESS AND BETTER LIFE

with Less Stress and More Productivity

MARY C. KELLY

PHD, CSP, COMMANDER, US NAVY (RET)

Weekly Guided Journal for Busy Professionals

© Copyright 2022 – Mary C. Kelly

All rights reserved. This book is protected by the copyright laws of the United States of America. No part of this publication may be reproduced, stored in or introduced into a retrieval system, or transmitted, in any form or by any means (electronic, mechanical, photocopying, recording or otherwise), without the prior written permission of the publisher. For permissions requests, contact the publisher, addressed "Attention: Permissions Coordinator," at the address below.

Published and Distributed by
SOUND WISDOM
PO Box 310
Shippensburg, PA 17257-0310
717-530-2122
info@soundwisdom.com
www.soundwisdom.com

While efforts have been made to verify information contained in this publication, neither the author nor the publisher assumes any responsibility for errors, inaccuracies, or omissions. While this publication is chock-full of useful, practical information, it is not intended to be legal or accounting advice. All readers are advised to seek competent lawyers and accountants to follow laws and regulations that may apply to specific situations. The reader of this publication assumes responsibility for the use of the information. The author and publisher assume no responsibility or liability whatsoever on the behalf of the reader of this publication.

The scanning, uploading and distribution of this publication via the Internet or via any other means without the permission of the publisher is illegal and punishable by law. Please purchase only authorized editions and do not participate in or encourage piracy of copyrightable materials.

ISBN 13 TP - 978-1-64095-417-5
ISBN 13 eBook - 978-1-64095-418-2

For Worldwide Distribution, Printed in the U.S.A.
1 2 3 4 5 6 / 22 21 20

INTRODUCTION

I grew up in a business family. I watched the progression from starting new businesses to growing businesses. I've seen the challenges experienced by leaders, entrepreneurs, and influencers who are trying to move their organizations forward.

In the Navy, if we do something more than a few times, we make a checklist for it. Similarly, before you get on a plane, you will notice the pilots walking around the plane with a checklist in their hands. They follow a checklist even if they've done it 1,000 times. Checklists prevent us from becoming complacent. Checklists ensure we are doing what we need to do, and they enable us to devote our time to other, higher-order things, such as creative thinking, because we know we have the basics covered. We don't have to worry that something fundamental is going to fall through the cracks, because it is on the checklist.

When I started working as a corporate advisor, it became clear to me that many businesses sometimes skip over important steps in their desire to grow. Many organizations, whether they are schools, churches, nonprofits, or mom-and-pop stores, oftentimes have the same struggles as Fortune 500 companies. They sometimes get so caught up in the day-to-day operations that they don't make the small course corrections necessary to make a big difference.

This is a collection of the resources I use all the time when working with my executive clients. Not every 5-Minute Plan will work for every person or every organization. However, I have yet to come across an organization that could not benefit from more focus within their teams, higher levels of productivity, targeted sales and marketing, better strategic planning, and employees who are loyal and engaged.

The areas of focus include:

1. **Business and organization planning**
2. **How to grow**
3. **Leading people**
4. **Personal development**
5. **Productivity**
6. **Teamwork**

The 5-Minute Plans are designed to help you focus on, improve, strengthen, and take action on the areas you need.

I encourage people to write in this guide and use it as a planner or journal.

Some of my leaders want to utilize the 5-Minute Plans for their entire team. To make that easy, all of the plans are accessible as fillable PDFs. There is a code included with the book. It is easy for anyone to get this book and share the topics collectively or individually with their teams.

I hope this book gives you the tools you need to make important and lasting changes both personally and professionally. I hope these tools help you strengthen your organization, create happier team members, and further your goals.

We have a complete video series that covers each one of these 5-Minute Plans, as well. It can be accessed by sending an email to **info@productiveleaders.com**.

Please feel free to reach out to me if you have any questions or would like a personal consultation. I wish you the very best of luck on your journey. I am cheering for you!

-Mary Kelly

SECTION 1

BUSINESS PLANNING

BETTER IN 52 WEEKS
ACTION STEPS TO A BETTER BUSINESS AND BETTER LIFE
with Less Stress and More Productivity

You cannot do a kindness too soon, for you never know how soon it will be too late.
~ RALPH WALDO EMERSON

My top priorities today are:

1. _____

2. _____

3. _____

Today's challenges include:

1. _____

2. _____

3. _____

Leadership skills I need to remember / practice today:

1. _____

2. _____

3. _____

I can encourage others to succeed if I:

1. _____

2. _____

3. _____

Today's accomplishments:

_____
_____
_____

Overall, today was:
○ Rough
○ Meh
○ Okay
○ Good
○ Great

From today's challenges I learned:

_____
_____

I can make tomorrow even better if I:

_____

5-MINUTE BUSINESS PLAN

Fill in the blanks/complete the sentences on this page to create a high-level business plan you can use right away.

1. The Big Picture/The Executive Summary

This identifies what we actually do and for whom.

We sell/provide _____
to people who _____

2. Making Life Better/Business Operations

In business we generally focus on filling a need, solving a problem, or improving someone's life somehow.

We are helping _____
We are increasing _____
We are reducing or getting rid of _____
_____

3. Profits/Financials

To be successful in business we have to make a profit. Making a profit means revenues are greater than expenses.

I charge _____
To get paid I _____
I can also earn money if I _____
_____

4. Almost Famous/Marketing

People need to know about us and our products or services.

Customers learn about us through _____
_____

Our social media plan includes _____
_____

We manage referrals by _____
_____

5. Climbing the Mountain/Management

You cannot do everything by ourselves. Outsource tasks or projects that can be accomplished easily by someone else.

I like doing _____
_____

I'll get help with _____
_____

6. Top of the World/Success

Know when we achieve goals. Celebrate milestones and accomplishments.

I'll know I'm successful when I have _____ (#) **customers, or sell** _____ (#) **products, or make $**_____ **income.**

Today, do what others won't, so tomorrow you can accomplish what others can't.
~ SIMONE BILES

My top priorities today are:

1. _____

2. _____

3. _____

Today's challenges include:

1. _____

2. _____

3. _____

Leadership skills I need to remember / practice today:

1. _____

2. _____

3. _____

I can encourage others to succeed if I:

1. _____

2. _____

3. _____

Today's accomplishments:

_____
_____
_____

Overall, today was:
○ Rough
○ Meh
○ Okay
○ Good
○ Great

From today's challenges I learned:

_____
_____

I can make tomorrow even better if I:

_____

5-MINUTE DIFFERENTIATION PLAN

How do we stand out? We need to be competitive in the market. Every car is exactly the same as every other vehicle on the road...except where it is different. That difference is what makes someone choose one make/model over another. The difference we provide is why people choose to work with us over someone else.

I am uniquely positioned because I am
(use words that are unique to you):

_____
_____
_____
_____
_____
_____

When people think about working with me I want them to think of these 3-6 characteristics:

1. _____
2. _____
3. _____
4. _____
5. _____
6. _____

My branding/marketing materials reflect these characteristics:

1	2	3	4	5
Not At All	A Bit	Sort Of	Mostly	Yes!

I can align my desired image characteristics by updating my:

- ○ Business card
- ○ Email signature
- ○ Professional headshot
- ○ Wardrobe
- ○ Social media presence
- ○ Performance at work
- ○ Interaction with clients

You are the only real obstacle in your path to a fulfilling life.

~ LES BROWN

My top priorities today are:

1. _____

2. _____

3. _____

Today's challenges include:

1. _____

2. _____

3. _____

Leadership skills I need to remember / practice today:

1. _____

2. _____

3. _____

I can encourage others to succeed if I:

1. _____

2. _____

3. _____

Today's accomplishments:

_____

_____

_____

Overall, today was:
- ○ Rough
- ○ Meh
- ○ Okay
- ○ Good
- ○ Great

From today's challenges I learned:

_____

_____

I can make tomorrow even better if I:

_____

5-MINUTE GOAL SETTING PLAN

Many people don't achieve their full potential because they don't define and work toward goals. When writing a goal, start with "I will" and assign a date for completion.

My Goal: _____   Completion Date: _____

I will: _____
_____
_____
_____

Obstacles
Goals are challenging for everyone, because everyone has obstacles. What are the obstacles? What are the solutions?

Obstacles	Solutions
1.	
2.	
3.	
4.	
5.	

Action Steps
What are 5 actions steps to make this goal a reality?

Action	Due Date	√
1.		
2.		
3.		
4.		
5.		

I will know I'm successful when...
_____
_____
_____

Reason and judgment are the qualities of a leader.
~ TACITUS

My top priorities today are:

1. _____
2. _____
3. _____

Today's challenges include:

1. _____
2. _____
3. _____

Leadership skills I need to remember / practice today:

1. _____
2. _____
3. _____

I can encourage others to succeed if I:

1. _____
2. _____
3. _____

Today's accomplishments:

_____
_____
_____

Overall, today was:
○ Rough
○ Meh
○ Okay
○ Good
○ Great

From today's challenges I learned:

_____
_____

I can make tomorrow even better if I:

_____

5-MINUTE ONLINE IMAGE PLAN

When people view us on social media platforms or our website, do they get a good sense of who we are? Are our values, differentiating characteristics, and personality evident? People work with us because they believe, like, and trust us. We need to make sure our online image cultivates that.

I can improve my online image by upgrading my online presence in these ways:

(check all that apply and note 1-2 changes to make)

- ○ Website
- ○ Website "about" section
- ○ Website photos
- ○ Website contact page
- ○ LinkedIn profile
- ○ LinkedIn articles
- ○ LinkedIn videos
- ○ LinkedIn shares / comments
- ○ Facebook profile
- ○ Facebook postings / shares / comments
- ○ Twitter profile
- ○ Twitter postings
- ○ Twitter retweets / comments
- ○ YouTube videos
- ○ Instagram profile
- ○ Instagram postings / comments
- ○ Pinterest profile
- ○ Pinterest postings
- ○ Pinterest categories

Made me learn a little bit faster. Made my skin a little bit thicker. Makes me that much smart. So thanks for making me a fighter.

~ CHRISTINA AGUILERA

My top priorities today are:

1. _____

2. _____

3. _____

Today's challenges include:

1. _____

2. _____

3. _____

Leadership skills I need to remember / practice today:

1. _____

2. _____

3. _____

I can encourage others to succeed if I:

1. _____

2. _____

3. _____

Today's accomplishments:

_____

_____

_____

Overall, today was:
- ○ Rough
- ○ Meh
- ○ Okay
- ○ Good
- ○ Great

From today's challenges I learned:

_____

_____

I can make tomorrow even better if I:

_____

5-MINUTE PRIORITIZATION PLAN

Many people find it difficult to prioritize work, so they procrastinate getting certain projects completed. This can be frustrating for the employee, the team, and their manager. Leaders can help people understand what is most important, and point them to what they need to focus on for mutual success.

We all know that often the urgent work ends up taking priority over the important tasks. We know the example of putting the big rocks in the jar first before the jar gets filled up with little rocks, sand, and water. But little tasks are often addressed first.

For managers and leaders:

Managers and leaders can help their people by asking:

"What are you working on today?"

"What are you working on this week?"

"Do you need any help on this project?"

"Are you familiar with the next project steps?"

Based on the answers, help the employee prioritize by providing a deadline and reason.

"Great! Our focus is on the Jones proposal right now, because they're making the decision on Friday afternoon. Can you have your part completed by Thursday at 8 a.m.?"

Further guide the time allocation with, *"The Jones project is our critical issue this week. Then we can move on to the Smith project."*

For employees:

Some employees work for supervisors who may not be great communicators. Rather than guessing, the key is to ask for clarification on information and deadlines.

"Susan, I want to do a great job on the Jones project. I know you need time to review it. What else do I need to know about the project?"

"Are there any deadlines I need to know about?"

"What do you need from me?"

I can better support the organization by focusing this week on:

1. _____
2. _____
3. _____
4. _____

Next week my top projects are:

1. _____
2. _____
3. _____
4. _____

*Freedom is actually a bigger game than power. Power is about what you can control.
Freedom is about what you can unleash.*

~ HARRIET RUBIN

My top priorities today are:

1. _____
2. _____
3. _____

Today's challenges include:

1. _____
2. _____
3. _____

Leadership skills I need to remember / practice today:

1. _____
2. _____
3. _____

I can encourage others to succeed if I:

1. _____
2. _____
3. _____

Today's accomplishments:

_____
_____
_____

Overall, today was:
○ Rough
○ Meh
○ Okay
○ Good
○ Great

From today's challenges I learned:

_____
_____

I can make tomorrow even better if I:

_____

5-MINUTE RECRUITING PLAN

Great leaders know that a key driver of success is a talented and motivated team of people who are a great fit for their roles. Attracting, engaging, and hiring talent is always challenging, and more so in today's complex and dynamic marketplace. How do we recruit wisely?

Take a lesson from the sports world!

How do you effectively recruit the talent you need for your organization—when competition is fierce, and there are so many variables both in your team and processes and the potential candidates?

Businesses can take a few lessons from sports recruiters.

What do sports recruiters do that business leaders and human resource professionals should remember?

1. They go where the talent is.
Where is my future talent?
Where do they currently live?
Where do they currently work?
_____
_____
_____
_____

2. They look for the potential.
What would my ideal candidate's potential look like?
What do I need to look for?
_____
_____
_____
_____

3. They plan for depth on the bench years in advance.
What talent, skills, and abilities will I need in 1, 3, and 5 years?
_____
_____
_____

Where do I have depth now?
_____
_____

What positions am I developing my employees for now?
_____
_____

4. They plan for contingencies because they know players can get hurt, be transferred, or not work out as well as they hoped.

Do I have a plan to replace people if they leave?
_____
_____
_____
_____

What positions in my organization are the most critical?
_____
_____
_____
_____

5. They're constantly scouting for talent.
When I find a great talent, how can I bring them into my organization?
_____
_____
_____
_____
_____

Wealth is the ability to fully experience life.
~ HENRY DAVID THOREAU

My top priorities today are:

1. _____
2. _____
3. _____

Today's challenges include:

1. _____
2. _____
3. _____

Leadership skills I need to remember / practice today:

1. _____
2. _____
3. _____

I can encourage others to succeed if I:

1. _____
2. _____
3. _____

Today's accomplishments:

_____
_____
_____

Overall, today was:
○ Rough
○ Meh
○ Okay
○ Good
○ Great

From today's challenges I learned:
_____
_____

I can make tomorrow even better if I:
_____

5-MINUTE STRATEGIC THINKING PLAN

Strategic thinking is about thinking big thoughts, looking toward the needs and products of the future, and crafting responsive plans needed to move forward. How can we help our teams think bigger? How do we think bigger? And how do we then focus our planning to effectively meet future possibilities and conditions?

Strategic thinking creates the capacity to plan for the future with attunement to changing environments and emerging challenges. This takes knowledge, skill, practice, and time.

1. See the big picture.

Know as much as possible about the organization and its people. Know what we do and whom we do it for.

We make/produce/provide _____
_____ **for** _____
_____.

2. Take time to reflect.

Great strategic thinkers "connect the dots"— people, ideas, and possibilities—and this requires time to reflect.

Some people think best with another person or people, while others need solitude. Either way, it requires time devoted to reflection and contemplation.

The best conditions for me to reflect deeply are _____
_____.

I brainstorm best with people who _____
_____.

3. Shift between and entertain different perspectives.

Strategic thinkers can tap into both divergent (big picture) and convergent (arranging the puzzle pieces) thinking, and they easily move between them to develop these skills. Try brainstorming with one other person at a time to view the issue from multiple perspectives.

I can brainstorm with _____
to gather information.

I can brainstorm with _____
to gauge how this issue is perceived.

I can brainstorm with _____
to figure out implementation.

I can brainstorm with _____
to see the issue from the outside.

4. Change your environment.

There is a reason many organizations hold "offsites." People need new environs, different stimuli, and to be "pleasantly uncomfortable" to shift thinking. We also need to eliminate distractions.

I can go to _____ **to think.**

My team could spend a day at _____
_____ **to think.**

5. Invest in cultivating strategy.

Some leaders hear strategic thinking initiatives and dismiss them as being frivolous. The future of the business and achieving long-term success depends on long-term strategy.

If there were no resource constraints, we could
_____.

If there was unlimited money, we could develop/ produce/incorporate/research/solve _____
_____.

It is not the mountains that we conquer, but ourselves.
~ SIR EDMUND HILLARY

My top priorities today are:

1. _____
2. _____
3. _____

Today's challenges include:

1. _____
2. _____
3. _____

Leadership skills I need to remember / practice today:

1. _____
2. _____
3. _____

I can encourage others to succeed if I:

1. _____
2. _____
3. _____

Today's accomplishments:

_____
_____
_____

Overall, today was:
○ Rough
○ Meh
○ Okay
○ Good
○ Great

From today's challenges I learned:

_____
_____

I can make tomorrow even better if I:

_____

5-MINUTE SUCCESSION PLAN

We know we need a succession plan. We're not going to live forever, and we want the chance to fish, golf, and travel. Our organization needs our knowledge, skills and abilities— and they also need to plan for a time when we're not there. Start working backwards. How can we prepare for when we are going to leave?

Assess the current roles and responsibilities of the position.

How has the position evolved?
_____
_____
_____

Is the job description still accurate?
_____
_____
_____

How will this job change in 3 to 5 years?
_____
_____
_____

What is the projected time for the current employee to leave?
_____
_____
_____

What likely challenges will the next leader face?
(i.e. mergers, acquisitions, foreign competition, new regulations, changing technology, evolving customer preferences, product placement, product development, employee talent development, etc.)
_____
_____
_____
_____

What leadership competencies and skills will the successor need?
Vital skills and competencies to evaluate:

- **Vision** – the ability to craft, communicate and engage others in long-term direction and goals.
- **Business judgment** – the ability to make sound and solid decisions that are in the best interest and long-term health of the company/organization.
- **Industry knowledge** – solid grasp of the history, current challenges and future opportunities of the industry. A strong network of both peers and influencers within the industry.
- **Strategic thinking** – the ability to think through challenges and opportunities, and develop and implement strategy.
- **Crisis management** – the ability to quickly analyze, grasp, understand and navigate through challenging times.
- **Financial acumen** – a strong understanding and expertise in financial matters both internal and external to the org.
- **Emotional intelligence** – the ability to easily understand, connect with, and adjust communication style to better relate to others
- **Influence** – the ability to motivate and inspire others to both self-organize and work together.
- **Conflict management** – the ability to immediately identify and address conflict, and help others work towards a peaceful solution.
- **Decision-making** – a proven track record of easily and effectively making and committing to decisions.
- **Interpersonal skills** – exhibiting skills that show you are respected and valued by the team.
- **Risk-taking** – the ability to take a chance and to make calculated risks.
- **Talent development** – the ability to attract, retain and fully develop top talent.

The best thing about the future is that it only comes one day at a time.
~ ABRAHAM LINCOLN

My top priorities today are:

1. _____
2. _____
3. _____

Today's challenges include:

1. _____
2. _____
3. _____

Leadership skills I need to remember / practice today:

1. _____
2. _____
3. _____

I can encourage others to succeed if I:

1. _____
2. _____
3. _____

Today's accomplishments:

_____
_____
_____

Overall, today was:
○ Rough
○ Meh
○ Okay
○ Good
○ Great

From today's challenges I learned:

_____
_____

I can make tomorrow even better if I:

_____

5-MINUTE VISION PLAN

Our mission is what we do, such as "we play baseball."
A vision is "we are going to the World Series."
Leaders need to create a vision that gives people purpose and direction,
and coalesces them around a goal bigger than themselves.

Before establishing the vision, we need to know our mission.

What do we actually do?
_____
_____
_____

Whom do we serve now?
_____
_____
_____

Think about the Really Big Picture to create the vision.

With a clearly understood mission, we can move into creating the vision.

Strategic thinking considers the big picture, potental changes, and every possible variable.

Whom will we serve in the future?

In 5 years?
_____

In 10 years?
_____

In 20 years?
_____

What major changes will we see in the future?
1. _____
2. _____
3. _____

How will these changes affect our purpose?
1. _____
2. _____
3. _____

What legacy do we want to leave? What do we want to be known for?
_____
_____
_____
_____

If there were no constraints, what would we do?
_____
_____
_____
_____

What is our vision?
_____
_____
_____
_____
_____

The greatest risk is the risk of riskless living.
~ STEPHEN R. COVEY

My top priorities today are:

1. _____
   _____
2. _____
   _____
3. _____
   _____

Today's challenges include:

1. _____
   _____
2. _____
   _____
3. _____
   _____

Leadership skills I need to remember / practice today:

1. _____
   _____
2. _____
   _____
3. _____
   _____

I can encourage others to succeed if I:

1. _____
   _____
2. _____
   _____
3. _____
   _____

Today's accomplishments:

_____
_____
_____

Overall, today was:
○ Rough
○ Meh
○ Okay
○ Good
○ Great

From today's challenges I learned:

_____
_____

I can make tomorrow even better if I:

_____

5-MINUTE WEBSITE PLAN

In today's intensely online world, having a website is necessary for nearly every business. Not having one makes it harder to be found. What's more, with over a billion websites on the Internet, ours needs to stand out.

On a scale of 1-3, where 1 is poor and 3 is fabulous, assign a number to assess how well we're doing and identify where we can improve. (1=poor, 2=okay, 3=fabulous)

____ Our website clearly communicates what we do/sell/provide

____ Our social media feeds are connected to our website to improve SEO

____ Our contact information, including phone number and address, are easy to find on the website

____ Our products are easily searchable on our website

____ It's easy to purchase from our website

____ Our website is searchable

____ We make it easy for people to sign up for updates/subscribe to newsletter

____ We have a mechanism for capturing information on current and future customers

____ Our website is current

____ Our website is constantly backed up

____ Our website is mobile-friendly

____ People browsing our site can easily find the information they need (and how do we know this? Focus group? Feedback? Testing?)

____ We run analytics monthly to improve site responsiveness

____ We are GDRP compliant and let people know we're collecting information using cookies

____ Our terms and conditions are clear

____ We offer a feedback mechanism

____ Our website reflects our brand well

SECTION 2

BUSINESS GROWTH

BETTER IN 52 WEEKS
ACTION STEPS TO A BETTER BUSINESS AND BETTER LIFE
with Less Stress and More Productivity

Passion is a huge prerequisite to winning.
~ KERRI WALSH JENNINGS

My top priorities today are:

1. _____
   _____
2. _____
   _____
3. _____
   _____

Today's challenges include:

1. _____
   _____
2. _____
   _____
3. _____
   _____

Leadership skills I need to remember / practice today:

1. _____
   _____
2. _____
   _____
3. _____
   _____

I can encourage others to succeed if I:

1. _____
   _____
2. _____
   _____
3. _____
   _____

Today's accomplishments:

_____
_____
_____

Overall, today was:
○ Rough
○ Meh
○ Okay
○ Good
○ Great

From today's challenges I learned:
_____
_____

I can make tomorrow even better if I:
_____

5-MINUTE BRAINSTORMING PLAN

Brainstorming with teams and groups is a highly effective way to generate ideas, get suggestions, and develop new offerings. Good leaders know that employees, staff, suppliers, and customers all have unique insights. They also recognize that people want to feel they have a voice in the future of an organization, and their thoughts are heard and valued.

Effective Brainstorming

Remember these points to leverage your brainstorming efforts most effectively.

Leaders speak last.

In a team meeting, leaders need to speak last, otherwise people perceive that leaders just want their own ideas validated.

Agree to be open and inclusive.

Before starting, people need to agree that there are no dumb ideas, that all ideas should be heard, and that everyone should contribute.

Capture ideas.

Ideas that are generated by brainstorming need to be captured in a way that are usable later. Many people use index cards or Post-it Notes® to quickly generate individual ideas, and then they sort them on a wall or large poster. It's also easy to record the meeting and have it transcribed.

Specificity creates relevance.

Questions for brainstorming need to be focused on a particular area so that ideas are as relevant as possible.

Overly general questions like "How can we improve the customer experience?" are not as good as specific questions such as:

1. How can we improve the customer experience in our retail store?
_____
_____

2. How can we improve the customer experience on our website?
_____
_____

3. How can we improve the experience when customers call us?
_____
_____

4. Where can we provide training for our emerging leaders?
_____
_____

5. What types of customers will we serve in 5 years?
_____
_____

6. What types of customers will we serve in 10 years?
_____
_____

Nothing happens unless first a dream.
~ CARL SANDBURG

My top priorities today are:

1. _____
2. _____
3. _____

Today's challenges include:

1. _____
2. _____
3. _____

Leadership skills I need to remember / practice today:

1. _____
2. _____
3. _____

I can encourage others to succeed if I:

1. _____
2. _____
3. _____

Today's accomplishments:

_____
_____
_____

Overall, today was:
- ○ Rough
- ○ Meh
- ○ Okay
- ○ Good
- ○ Great

From today's challenges I learned:

_____
_____

I can make tomorrow even better if I:

_____

5-MINUTE BUSINESS GROWTH PLAN

Growing a business involves thousands of details. Sometimes we need to take a step back to discern what will take us to the next level. This assessment identifies where you're strong, what needs attention, and how to proceed.

We have a business plan that accurately describes our business.
○ Yes ○ Maybe ○ Not Sure ○ No

We have a strategic vision for our business that is driving us toward future success.
○ Yes ○ Maybe ○ Not Sure ○ No

Everyone is clear on our goals for moving the organization forward.
○ Yes ○ Maybe ○ Not Sure ○ No

We know our break-even points, as well as our total revenue, total cost, and profits.
○ Yes ○ Maybe ○ Not Sure ○ No

We have systems in place for actively generating, receiving, and thanking referrals.
○ Yes ○ Maybe ○ Not Sure ○ No

We have systems in place to show customers our appreciation for their business.
○ Yes ○ Maybe ○ Not Sure ○ No

We have systems in place for getting honest feedback.
○ Yes ○ Maybe ○ Not Sure ○ No

Our website is easy to navigate.
○ Yes ○ Maybe ○ Not Sure ○ No

Our website is mobile friendly.
○ Yes ○ Maybe ○ Not Sure ○ No

Our social media is updated consistently and linked to our website.
○ Yes ○ Maybe ○ Not Sure ○ No

Our website can capture customer contact information.
○ Yes ○ Maybe ○ Not Sure ○ No

We have trusted advisors to keep us on track such as a corporate advisor, board of directors, or a mastermind.
○ Yes ○ Maybe ○ Not Sure ○ No

We devote resources to professional training for our team.
○ Yes ○ Maybe ○ Not Sure ○ No

Everyone on our team knows how to take great care of our customers.
○ Yes ○ Maybe ○ Not Sure ○ No

We follow up with our clients the way we should.
○ Yes ○ Maybe
○ Not Sure ○ No

The achievements of an organization are the results of the combined effort of each individual.
~ VINCE LOMBARDI

My top priorities today are:

1. _____
   _____
2. _____
   _____
3. _____
   _____

Today's challenges include:

1. _____
   _____
2. _____
   _____
3. _____
   _____

Leadership skills I need to remember / practice today:

1. _____
   _____
2. _____
   _____
3. _____
   _____

I can encourage others to succeed if I:

1. _____
   _____
2. _____
   _____
3. _____
   _____

Today's accomplishments:

_____
_____
_____

Overall, today was:
- ○ Rough
- ○ Meh
- ○ Okay
- ○ Good
- ○ Great

From today's challenges I learned:

_____
_____

I can make tomorrow even better if I:

_____

5-MINUTE CUSTOMER SERVICE PLAN

The best businesses are laser-focused on current and future needs of their customers and other economic buyers. Really great companies understand Say's Law: supply creates its own demand for terrific products and services. We also have to deliver service and experiences in a way that exceeds current customer expectations.

Answer these questions honestly to explore where your business can improve.

Our customers are wowed by every interaction with this organization.
____ Yes! We're at the top of our game!
____ Maybe
____ Not so much

How can we find ways to improve from the customer's point of view?
____ Focus groups
____ Polls
____ Incentivized surveys
____ Phone calls
____ Other
_____
_____
_____

If we improved our customer's experience, what would that do for the organization?
1. _____
2. _____
3. _____

Where can we improve the customer experience?
1. _____
2. _____
3. _____

What parts of the buying process stop customers from proceeding with the purchase?
____ First introduction to the product or service
____ Website links
____ Understanding the product's/service's benefits
____ Actual purchase process

How can we provide additional information/service/value throughout the process?

Our customers commit to us when we...
_____
_____
_____

Our follow-up for our clients is
____ Fabulous!
____ Not great
____ Cringe-worthy

We can improve our follow-up by:
1. _____
2. _____
3. _____

What can we provide to our clients that adds value for them:
1. _____
2. _____
3. _____

Find out who you are and do it on purpose.
~ DOLLY PARTON

My top priorities today are:

1. _____
2. _____
3. _____

Today's challenges include:

1. _____
2. _____
3. _____

Leadership skills I need to remember / practice today:

1. _____
2. _____
3. _____

I can encourage others to succeed if I:

1. _____
2. _____
3. _____

Today's accomplishments:

_____
_____
_____

Overall, today was:
○ Rough
○ Meh
○ Okay
○ Good
○ Great

From today's challenges I learned:

_____
_____

I can make tomorrow even better if I:

_____

5-MINUTE
GIVE-UP-GOOD-TO-GET-TO-GREAT PLAN

It is difficult to abandon what's comfortable and relatively good to become uncomfortable in the hopes of becoming great. It may feel like stepping off a cliff. Yet often, that's what it takes. As leaders, we have to find ways to help others push beyond their comfort zones.

Status quo is a comfortable place. We know what we need to do to be fairly successful. We may be comfortable in our jobs, confident in what we know, and performing well.

But the world is changing quickly. Businesses that do not continually improve will wind up stagnating and become obsolete, like the 8-track tape player.

We have to give up good to get to great. That means as leaders, we have to help others explore options and take risks. We have to give up what is merely good today to achieve greatness in the future.

Who or what is holding me back from my full potential?
Who: _____
_____

What: _____
_____

Why is it challenging to get rid of the issues, situations, or people who are holding me back?
_____
_____
_____
_____

Are these obstacles speed bumps or mountains?

Obstacle   *Speed Bump or Mountain*

_____
_____
_____
_____
_____
_____
_____

What do I need to stop doing, because I am holding myself back?
1. _____
2. _____
3. _____
4. _____

What does my "GREAT" look like?
_____
_____
_____
_____
_____
_____
_____
_____
_____

When the flower blooms, the bees come uninvited.
~ RAMA KRISHNA

My top priorities today are:

1. _____
2. _____
3. _____

Today's challenges include:

1. _____
2. _____
3. _____

Leadership skills I need to remember / practice today:

1. _____
2. _____
3. _____

I can encourage others to succeed if I:

1. _____
2. _____
3. _____

Today's accomplishments:

_____
_____
_____

Overall, today was:
○ Rough
○ Meh
○ Okay
○ Good
○ Great

From today's challenges I learned:
_____
_____

I can make tomorrow even better if I:
_____

5-MINUTE FOLLOW-UP PLAN

We need to stay in touch with people we currently do business with, those we've done business with in the past, and those we hope to do business with in the future. If you've ever come home from a networking event or conference with a pile of business cards and then done nothing with them, this may help.

Important keys to effective follow-up:

- Whatever outreach you decide to do, remember that most people need several touch points before they think seriously about working with you.

- When you follow up, make sure the correspondence is about *them*—not you!

- Show a genuine interest in being helpful.

Great ways to follow up:

Follow up with people you want to stay in touch with by:

1. Mailing a handwritten note (and include your business card).

2. Sending a note using a service like SendOutCards.

3. Forwarding an article or video that may be of business interest to them.

4. Ordering a business-oriented book they may appreciate, and letting them know to expect a package in the mail.

5. Connecting with them on LinkedIn or other social platforms. Include a brief but friendly note that reminds them of something you discussed when you met.

6. Asking them if you can add them to your outreach initiative list or CRM. (It's important to ask permission for this, as automatically adding people to your mailing list is considered spam.)

7. Finding someone you both know, and starting an online conversation with the three of you.

8. Discovering common interests, and sending a message highlighting that commonality:

"Sam, I think we were in Minnesota at the same time—you were at U of M, while I was at 3M!"

9. Calling to say it was nice to meet them. (Yes—actually using the phone!)

10. Sending a short video.

11. Sending a short voice memo attached to an email with a follow-up to your conversation.

12. Sending a link for helpful resource material, and then following up with a note asking if they were able to access the materials.

13. Offering a short discovery conversation or consultation to offer a taste of your work or services.

14. Inviting them for coffee to get to know each other's work further.

15. Initiating a video conference virtual "coffee" or happy hour to catch up.

It's your attitude not your aptitude that determines your altitude.
~ ZIG ZIGLAR

My top priorities today are:

1. _____

2. _____

3. _____

Today's challenges include:

1. _____

2. _____

3. _____

Leadership skills I need to remember / practice today:

1. _____

2. _____

3. _____

I can encourage others to succeed if I:

1. _____

2. _____

3. _____

Today's accomplishments:

_____
_____
_____

Overall, today was:
- ○ Rough
- ○ Meh
- ○ Okay
- ○ Good
- ○ Great

From today's challenges I learned:

_____
_____

I can make tomorrow even better if I:

_____

5-MINUTE MARKETING PLAN

Every business needs to communicate what they do and who benefits from their products and services. Many businesses practice "spray and pray marketing" or the "shotgun" approach, where they send out promotions without targeting a niche or message. Marketing to "everyone" wastes resources.

Marketing dollars need to focus on the people who want and can buy our products.

Ideal clients

We all love working with clients who appreciate our products and services. We need to make sure we're targeting our ideal clients with clear focus. That means knowing who they are, what they want/need, where they "live" (literally and figuratively), and how to address their issues.

We love working with:
_____
_____

Because they:
_____
_____

They want/like:
_____
_____

We find them by:
_____
_____

We keep in touch with them with by:
_____
_____

Our top clients know we care about them because we:
_____
_____

Communicating

Are we communicating with our clients enough? And in the right ways?

Ideally, our communication should be informative, interesting, consistent, and helpful. **How often do our clients hear from us?**

Our methods of communicating with our customers usually need to include several "touch" points.

On a scale of 1-5, where 1 is poor and 5 is fabulous, assign a number to assess how well we are doing to identify where we can improve.

Which of these, if we improved, would benefit us and our customers the most? Mark that one.

____ Emails   ____ Phone calls
____ Newsletters   ____ Advertisements
____ Flyers   ____ Mailers
____ Face-to-face meetings
____ Meals/Entertainment
____ Video conferencing, such as Zoom or Skype
____ Other _____

Prioritize

If you had an extra $10,000 to spend on marketing, where would you spend it?
_____
_____
_____
_____
_____
_____

*The very essence of leadership is that you have to have vision.
You can't blow an uncertain trumpet.*

~ THEODORE M. HESBURGH

My top priorities today are:

1. _____
2. _____
3. _____

Today's challenges include:

1. _____
2. _____
3. _____

Leadership skills I need to remember / practice today:

1. _____
2. _____
3. _____

I can encourage others to succeed if I:

1. _____
2. _____
3. _____

Today's accomplishments:

_____
_____
_____

Overall, today was:
○ Rough
○ Meh
○ Okay
○ Good
○ Great

From today's challenges I learned:

_____
_____

I can make tomorrow even better if I:

_____

5-MINUTE NETWORKING PLAN

The goal of networking is finding others to do business with. Many people find networking events challenging—even extroverts! Online forums and social media can help, but there is still a need for face-to-face conversations and live social gatherings. How can we effectively navigate networking events?

Some people love talking with strangers, getting to know them, and learning about their work and business. Others know they should network, but the thought of walking into a room full of strangers and making small talk makes a root canal sound like a better way to spend the afternoon. Even for extroverts, networking can be challenging.

Here are some ways to make the most of networking events.

1. Prepare in advance. Have a focused plan. Is there a particular person you want to meet? A particular client profile you are looking for? Be clear about why you are attending a function.

2. Look the part. Don't think you can stop by a business networking event after playing softball without changing clothes. Look like the professional you are.

3. Bring a pen, and use it. When you meet someone and exchange cards (yes, people still use actual business cards) write down on their card where you met them and what you're going to do to follow up. We all have piles of business cards that we don't know what to do with because we didn't make notes at the time.

4. Bring business cards. Make your business cards stand out. I have a friend in real estate who specializes in properties for older people, and part of her card is a magnifying glass. No one throws away her card, and it instantly brands her.

5. Network with a friend. Go to the event with a trusted friend. Introduce and promote each other. It's easier for people to believe other people talking about how great you are than you telling people how great you are.

Here's the difference:
"Hi Jane! I'm John Doe and I am an AMAZING insurance agent! You can trust me to do what is right for your family because, even though I just met you, I really care about you!"

Versus:
"Hi! Nice to meet you! Have you met John Doe? John is my insurance agent and he's amazing at assessing what I need. Insurance can be really complicated and expensive if you don't have the right agent watching out for you. I totally trust him to figure out what I need. John, do you have a card you can give to Jane?"

6. Focus on others. It's really easy to slide into our own elevator speech, hoping that the other person finds us fascinating and wants to work with us. What works even better is focusing on the other person. Great networkers know that people like talking about themselves, so ask questions and listen for answers.

7. Smile. It sounds basic, but many people allow anxiety and their surroundings to make them tense. Smile when talking with others. Be happy to see them and to listen.

8. Mingle. People are at a networking event to network, so don't get trapped into just talking with your friends or just one person.

9. Say thank you for their time. As you move to another group of people, thank the group you are leaving.

10. Schedule time to follow up. You got dressed, you went to the event, and you made some good contacts. FOLLOW UP! Most people don't. If you go to all of the trouble to go to the event and don't follow up, then you wasted your time and theirs. Schedule time during the day or two afterwards to follow up.

Take it slow. It'll work itself out just fine.
All we need is just a little patience.
~ GUNS N' ROSES

My top priorities today are:

1. _____
2. _____
3. _____

Today's challenges include:

1. _____
2. _____
3. _____

Leadership skills I need to remember / practice today:

1. _____
2. _____
3. _____

I can encourage others to succeed if I:

1. _____
2. _____
3. _____

Today's accomplishments:

_____
_____
_____

Overall, today was:
- ○ Rough
- ○ Meh
- ○ Okay
- ○ Good
- ○ Great

From today's challenges I learned:
_____
_____

I can make tomorrow even better if I:
_____

5-MINUTE SALES PLAN

Everyone in every organization is in sales. Every time you represent yourself or your organization, you are conveying value. Sales is helping people find solutions to their needs.

Most sales specialists agree that the most effective sales transactions are those where both parties feel like they are better off.

Great salespeople know to:

1. Research the customer's needs.

Know their business, their industry, their competition, and their core issues.

2. Focus on the customer.

Ask clarifying, specific, and smart questions.

3. Suggest the right solutions for the customer's needs.

What do I or my products do to solve my customer's problem?

One of the best pieces of advice I ever got was from my dad at a trade show. I had a couple willing to buy a full case of items when they really only wanted half. My dad said, "Never sell what they don't want."

Almost everyone else is going to try to upsell. When you give people exactly what they want, they remember that. No one likes being oversold.

4. Acknowledge the challenges and provide options.

Hopefully, you are the solution, but sometimes you may not be. In that case, know your competition well enough to know when they are a better fit for your customer. Refer your customer to the right source and facilitate the introduction. Again—they will remember.

5. See the issue from the customer's perspective.

Be relatable, empathetic, and genuine. No one likes to be sold to, but people like buying. Put yourself in their shoes. How would I feel if I had this issue?

6. Agree to work together.

The best transactions are viewed as partnerships. "I am excited to be your partner as we move forward with _____."

7. Follow up.

The sales process does not end once the transaction is completed. Stay in touch!

Erase the word 'failure' from your vocabulary.
~ MARY LOU RETTON

My top priorities today are:

1. _____
   _____
2. _____
   _____
3. _____
   _____

Today's challenges include:

1. _____
   _____
2. _____
   _____
3. _____
   _____

Leadership skills I need to remember / practice today:

1. _____
   _____
2. _____
   _____
3. _____
   _____

I can encourage others to succeed if I:

1. _____
   _____
2. _____
   _____
3. _____
   _____

Today's accomplishments:

_____
_____
_____

Overall, today was:
○ Rough
○ Meh
○ Okay
○ Good
○ Great

From today's challenges I learned:

_____
_____

I can make tomorrow even better if I:

_____

5-MINUTE SOCIAL MEDIA PLAN

Manage your social media reputation by being consistent. Be entertaining, informative, and interesting. Focus on providing great content on the social media sites visited by your clients and customers.

Commitment/Consistency

I will participate in _____ (social media platforms, such as LinkedIn, Facebook, Twitter, Instagram, YouTube, etc.) which is where my business/clients are.

I will post an interesting article or comment on_____ (my main topics of expertise) at least ___ times per day.

I will share an article or video or picture or quote on a social media platform such as Twitter, Facebook, LinkedIn, YouTube, Google+, Instagram (circle one) at least ___ times per day.

LinkedIn — Knowing Me, Knowing You

Establish your professional resume, including a picture. When LinkedIn sends you a notification that someone has recommended or endorsed you, respond.

Send replies to people who connect with and message you.

To expand your network, invite connections.

I will send ____ invitations to connect with people within my sphere of influence every week.

I will post an interesting article to at least ____ LinkedIn groups once a week.

I will endorse ____ (# of) people at least ___ times per week.

Facebook/Group or Page

Facebook is used by businesspeople to create interest in and share information about their products and services. Actively engage others by commenting on their Facebook pages, clicking on "likes," and being supportive.

I will post at least ___ times per day.

I will comment on other people's posts/comments at least ___ times per day.

Twitter — Not Angry Birds

Using Twitter to unite groups can be powerful. Use hashtags for best search engine optimizations.

Tweet current information, helpful promotions, or entertaining pictures. If someone read your last 5 tweets, would they know what to do?

I will tweet at least ____ times per week.

I will respond to all direct messages within ____ day(s).

Pinterest — More Than Recipes

You can create categories that are interesting to your clients, or you can profile your clients on your Pinterest account. People like attention; having content repinned is flattering.

I will create a category called _____ that will be interesting to my customer base.

Social media is social, after all, so while you are using it for business, stay friendly and authentic.

Be bold, be bold, and everywhere be bold.
~ HERBERT SPENCER

My top priorities today are:

1. _____

2. _____

3. _____

Today's challenges include:

1. _____

2. _____

3. _____

Leadership skills I need to remember / practice today:

1. _____

2. _____

3. _____

I can encourage others to succeed if I:

1. _____

2. _____

3. _____

Today's accomplishments:

_____
_____
_____

Overall, today was:
○ Rough
○ Meh
○ Okay
○ Good
○ Great

From today's challenges I learned:

_____
_____

I can make tomorrow even better if I:

_____

5-MINUTE WORK POTENTIAL PLAN

When we're not working to our full potential, we may feel stuck in a job, relationship, or a location. This can cause us to doubt our value and can manifest as irritability, frustration at work over trivial matters, and being easily angered. In reality, we're angry with ourselves for not living up to our full potential. The solution is to act on that potential—but how?

How do we make changes to reach our highest potential?

Should we stay in our current position? _____
Should we stay with the current organization? _____
How do we get the job we want? _____
Spend a few minutes thoughtfully and honestly answering these questions:

Am I currently in the job I want?
1   2   3   4   5
No   Maybe   Yes

Do the people I work with value me?
1   2   3   4   5
No   Maybe   Yes

Does my direct supervisor appreciate me?
1   2   3   4   5
No   Maybe   Yes

This job could be better if I...
_____
_____

This job could be better if my boss...
_____
_____

Does this job challenge me?
1   2   3   4   5
No   Maybe   Yes

What challenges do I enjoy in this job?
1. _____
2. _____
3. _____
4. _____

What aspects of this job give me satisfaction?
1. _____
2. _____
3. _____
4. _____

Would I be happier in another job at this company?
1   2   3   4   5
No   Maybe   Yes

What other positions am I interested in with this organization?
_____
_____

What positions am I interested in with another organization?
_____
_____

If I am going to leave this organization, what do I need to do?
- ○ Network better outside of work
- ○ Improve performance
- ○ Explore other opportunities
- ○ Update skill set

If I am going to stay at this organization, I need to:
- ○ Find out about other opportunities at this organization
- ○ Network better at work
- ○ Improve my attitude
- ○ Have an honest discussion with my supervisor about opportunities here
- ○ Recommit to being a great employee

The results you achieve will be in direct proportion to the effort you apply.
~ DENIS WAITLEY

My top priorities today are:

1. _____

2. _____

3. _____

Today's challenges include:

1. _____

2. _____

3. _____

Leadership skills I need to remember / practice today:

1. _____

2. _____

3. _____

I can encourage others to succeed if I:

1. _____

2. _____

3. _____

Today's accomplishments:

_____

_____

_____

Overall, today was:
- ○ Rough
- ○ Meh
- ○ Okay
- ○ Good
- ○ Great

From today's challenges I learned:

_____

_____

I can make tomorrow even better if I:

_____

5-MINUTE YEAR-IN-REVIEW PLAN

Assessing the past year helps us plan for the future. Now is a great time to finish old business so we can move forward. As we move into a new year, acknowledge past accomplishments as well as challenges.

In 3 words, describe business in the past year. _____, _____, _____.

In 3 words, describe my personal life/health in the past year. _____, _____, _____.

In 3 words, describe my personal relationships in the past year. _____, _____, _____.

Describe 3 things I worried about last year that I don't need to consider this year.
1. _____
2. _____
3. _____

What was the best decision I made last year?
_____
_____
_____

What helped make me successful?
_____
_____
_____

What was my biggest accomplishment last year?
_____
_____
_____

What 3 people can I thank for helping me last year?
1. _____
2. _____
3. _____

What unfinished business is still left from last year?
_____
_____
_____

What was the low point of last year?
_____
_____
_____

What can I do to avoid that in the future?
_____
_____
_____

Whom can I work with/ask for help/mentor this next year?
_____
_____
_____

What is my top goal for the next year?
_____
_____
_____

What top three actions can I take to make that goal a reality?
1. _____
2. _____
3. _____

SECTION 3

LEADING PEOPLE

BETTER IN 52 WEEKS
ACTION STEPS TO A BETTER
BUSINESS AND BETTER LIFE
with Less Stress and More Productivity

Problems are to the mind what exercise is to the muscles, they toughen and make strong.
~ NORMAN VINCENT PEALE

My top priorities today are:

1. _____

2. _____

3. _____

Today's challenges include:

1. _____

2. _____

3. _____

Leadership skills I need to remember / practice today:

1. _____

2. _____

3. _____

I can encourage others to succeed if I:

1. _____

2. _____

3. _____

Today's accomplishments:

_____

_____

_____

Overall, today was:
- ○ Rough
- ○ Meh
- ○ Okay
- ○ Good
- ○ Great

From today's challenges I learned:

_____

_____

I can make tomorrow even better if I:

_____

5-MINUTE CAREER PLAN

We can keep our careers moving in a positive, productive direction by devoting just a few minutes to these insightful questions. We need to help other people further their careers as well, in ways that encourage them to do more of what they are intrinsically motivated to do.

Passion
I get excited when I talk about:
1. _____
2. _____
3. _____

Energy
Working on:
_____
_____
_____
_____ gives me energy.

Focus
My perfect workday involves me completing:
1. _____
2. _____
3. _____

Satisfaction
The best part of my week happens when:
_____
_____
_____
_____
_____

Moving Forward
I can move my career forward at this job by doing more _____,
interacting with _____
and asking _____
for help.

Pay It Forward
I can help other people with their business or their career if:
_____
_____
_____
_____
_____
_____
_____
_____

Our chief want in life is somebody who shall make us do what we can.
~ RALPH WALDO EMERSON

My top priorities today are:

1. _____
_____

2. _____
_____

3. _____
_____

Today's challenges include:

1. _____
_____

2. _____
_____

3. _____
_____

Leadership skills I need to remember / practice today:

1. _____
_____

2. _____
_____

3. _____
_____

I can encourage others to succeed if I:

1. _____
_____

2. _____
_____

3. _____
_____

Today's accomplishments:

_____
_____
_____

Overall, today was:
○ Rough
○ Meh
○ Okay
○ Good
○ Great

From today's challenges I learned:

_____
_____

I can make tomorrow even better if I:

_____

5-MINUTE CHANGE MANAGEMENT PLAN

Most people find change difficult. How can we as leaders and managers help our people who are experiencing change? We start by exploring how people react to change, understanding their perspective, and then helping them move into the exploration and commitment phase.

What words describe how most people feel about change?

_____
_____
_____
_____

When faced with a change, most people react negatively and may make comments like:

_____
_____
_____
_____
_____

Why don't most people like change? Change means:

_____
_____

which can be:

_____
_____

Some people love change. These people find change to be:

_____
_____
_____
_____

Changing how we see change

Thinking about what happens if we don't change can get us excited about the possibilities of the future.

If we don't change, we become:

_____
_____
_____
_____
_____

Leaders can help their teams by focusing on the necessity and the positive outcomes of the change.

Leaders need to stay focused on the vision and the mission.

The J-Curve of Change
Transition Phases

Denial
"My boss can't leave."

"I'm not reporting to someone else."

Resistance
"Why would they do that?"
"This will never work."

Commitment
"Growth requires change."

"We can make this work together."

Exploration
"Are there are upsides?"

"Maybe this will work if..."

Failure is nature's plan to prepare you for great responsibilities.
~ NAPOLEON HILL

My top priorities today are:

1. _____
2. _____
3. _____

Today's challenges include:

1. _____
2. _____
3. _____

Leadership skills I need to remember / practice today:

1. _____
2. _____
3. _____

I can encourage others to succeed if I:

1. _____
2. _____
3. _____

Today's accomplishments:

_____
_____
_____

Overall, today was:
- ○ Rough
- ○ Meh
- ○ Okay
- ○ Good
- ○ Great

From today's challenges I learned:

_____
_____

I can make tomorrow even better if I:

_____

5-MINUTE CONFLICT RESOLUTION PLAN

We all experience disagreements, even with (especially with!) people close to us. Disagreements are natural, and sometimes necessary, to spur innovation, but we need to manage conflict so it remains positive and creative instead of negative and angry.

5 Steps to Resolve Conflict

1. Discuss a collaborative, positive vision of the desired future outcome.
"We all want to make sure this project goes forward."

Positively state the future outcome of your conflict:
_____
_____
_____
_____

2. Articulate the problem.
"Departments are habitually late providing reports to accounting."

Factually state the basis of the conflict:
_____
_____
_____
_____

3. Factually show why this is a problem.
"When accounting cannot get inputs from all of the departments on time, we lose our supplier bonus."

State the impact of the unresolved issue:
_____
_____
_____
_____

4. Ask for positive solutions.
"Make deadlines clearer."
"Reward the departments who are early."

Detail a possible positive solution:
_____
_____
_____
_____
_____

5. End positively.
"Thanks, everyone, for figuring out a way to fix this."

What words might be used to encourage people to move forward?
_____
_____
_____
_____
_____

"Fix the problem, not the blame."
— *Japanese Proverb*

To exist is to change, to change is to mature, to mature is to go on creating oneself endlessly.

~ HENRI BERGSON

My top priorities today are:

1. _____
2. _____
3. _____

Today's challenges include:

1. _____
2. _____
3. _____

Leadership skills I need to remember / practice today:

1. _____
2. _____
3. _____

I can encourage others to succeed if I:

1. _____
2. _____
3. _____

Today's accomplishments:

_____
_____
_____

Overall, today was:
- ○ Rough
- ○ Meh
- ○ Okay
- ○ Good
- ○ Great

From today's challenges I learned:

_____

I can make tomorrow even better if I:

_____

5-MINUTE DELEGATION PLAN

Many managers and leaders struggle to delegate. It's hard to relinquish control. When delegating, we retain the responsibility for getting that task accomplished—we're supervising the process.

We cannot and should not do everything ourselves.

1. We don't have unlimited time.
2. We don't have unlimited talent. Other people may do some things better than we can.
3. Others may have a lower opportunity cost for doing a specific job.

Calculate opportunity cost.

Opportunity is the highest, best use of our time. A lost opportunity has a cost, and it needs to be calculated.

Every time we make a decision to spend time doing one thing, we forego the opportunity to do something else. If that something else could be making us money—or in some other way "paying" us in rest, energy, pleasure, restoration or creativity—then it's worth considering.

Say we decide to go skiing, foregoing 8 hours of the opportunity to deliver pizza at $20 an hour. The cost of skiing for 8 hours is not just the cost of renting skis, the lift pass, and transportation. It's the cost of what we could be doing, but won't be—in this case delivering pizza. That $160 of lost opportunity needs to be considered.

If we can hire someone to do a task at a lower opportunity cost than our own, then we should. For example, we may know how to change the oil in the car, but auto service companies can do it more efficiently and at a much lower opportunity cost than we can.

I should delegate:
1. _____
2. _____
3. _____

Tips for delegation when you have employees:

Remember, we're not *reliquishing control*. We still own the responsibility for that task; we're just not doing it. Supervising can take less energy. To make it go smoothly:

1. Delegate to someone who has a natural skill.
2. Delegate to someone who wants to enhance their skills, or wants to learn a new skill.
3. Delegate to someone whose role dictates that they do that job.

Tips for delegation when you DON'T have employees (or are one):

Many people protest that they cannot delegate because their company will not pay for outsourcing or extra help. So we need to pay for it ourselves. If we struggle with making a flyer or creating a brochure, or some other job that can be outsourced, outsourcing it frees up time to focus on the parts of the job that we enjoy.

Some tips:
1. Trade jobs with another co-worker because they can do it better, or because it is a task you just don't want to do.
2. Outsource jobs (assuming no privacy issues are involved) via virtual services such as: FancyHands.com, Fiverr.com, or Upwork.
3. Hire part-time help at nights or on weekends to help you get work done.
4. Get a virtual assistant.

I will delegate:
1. _____
2. _____
3. _____

If you don't think every day is a good day, just try missing one.
~ CAVETT ROBERT

My top priorities today are:

1. _____
   _____
2. _____
   _____
3. _____
   _____

Today's challenges include:

1. _____
   _____
2. _____
   _____
3. _____
   _____

Leadership skills I need to remember / practice today:

1. _____
   _____
2. _____
   _____
3. _____
   _____

I can encourage others to succeed if I:

1. _____
   _____
2. _____
   _____
3. _____
   _____

Today's accomplishments:

_____
_____
_____

Overall, today was:
- ○ Rough
- ○ Meh
- ○ Okay
- ○ Good
- ○ Great

From today's challenges I learned:

_____
_____

I can make tomorrow even better if I:

_____

5-MINUTE FEEDBACK PLAN

Most people dislike official performance evaluations. Supervisors procrastinate on doing them, and employees dread them. Yet feedback is critical for us to improve. We need guidance and direction. Waiting until the mandatory yearly performance meeting is ineffective. Great leaders provide more feedback, more often, and in a way that motivates the receiver to perform even better.

How can leaders and managers today incorporate effective feedback into their organizations? Here are ways to provide better feedback:

1. Provide feedback more often. Schedule a time to personally praise, encourage, or thank each person.

I can provide feedback to _____
about _____ .

2. Focus on the project, not on the individual.
Use phrases like:
- "We need to expand the parameters to include this."
- "The client wants this section revised."
- "Can this be done with these changes?"

3. Redirect time and focus with phrases like:
- "I know you enjoy working on the Jones project. But our most important project this week is the Smith project, so please focus on that deadline. Thanks!"

4. Provide deadlines. People work to deadlines, so give them deadlines.
- "We need this completed by Friday at 2:00 PM, because our meeting with the client is at 3:00 PM."

5. Create 2-way conversations. Instead of giving a directive, have a casual conversation. When employees are engaged in conversation, they're more comfortable, and are more open to the topic.

TIP: Have them speak first about a problem or situation. Ask questions that elicit information, such as:
- "What do you think is going well on this project?"
- "Where do you think we can improve this project?"
- "If you were in charge of this, what would you do differently?"

6. Sometimes we need to address specific behaviors. Use specific examples for clarity. Generalizations such as "You are not reliable" are not helpful. Broach topics clearly and in a helpful manner to improve performance.

TRY:
- "This is the third time you've been late this week. Is there something I can help with?"
- "This project deadline was yesterday afternoon. Are there obstacles I should know about?"

7. Make sure to let people know when they are doing a great job. When praising people, make sure to be specific about what they did right.

- "Thanks for taking care of that difficult customer. You stayed really calm and they left with a good solution."
- "You did a great job handling the negotiations on that contract. That was better than we expected. Here is a bonus."
- "Thank you for running the meeting. People said you assigned projects well and they're excited about being on your team."

You should never stay at the same level. Always push yourself to the next.

~ MARNELLI DIMZON

My top priorities today are:

1. _____
2. _____
3. _____

Today's challenges include:

1. _____
2. _____
3. _____

Leadership skills I need to remember / practice today:

1. _____
2. _____
3. _____

I can encourage others to succeed if I:

1. _____
2. _____
3. _____

Today's accomplishments:

_____
_____
_____

Overall, today was:
○ Rough
○ Meh
○ Okay
○ Good
○ Great

From today's challenges I learned:

_____
_____

I can make tomorrow even better if I:

_____

5-MINUTE LEADERSHIP IMPROVEMENT PLAN

The most effective leaders are constantly seeking to improve themselves. It is easy to get complacent, especially when you're successful. But if we're not improving and expanding, we remain at status quo, or we are getting worse. Continuous improvement takes commitment, focus, and effort.

What can I improve that would make me a better leader for my direct reports/teams?
_____
_____
_____
_____

My direct reports say I'd be an even better supervisor if:
_____
_____
_____
_____

Being a great leader means being a better worker.

How can I support my coworkers to help them be more successful at their jobs?
_____
_____
_____
_____

How can I be more supportive of my boss?
_____
_____
_____
_____

What are some possible areas for improvement?

Ideas may include:
- Communication
- Encouragement
- Building teams
- Budgeting
- Social Media
- Email management/clarity
- Managing expectations
- Advertising
- Branding
- Providing feedback
- Customer contact
- Marketing
- Sales
- Listening
- Industry knowledge
- Policies
- Strategic planning
- Conflict resolution

My best means of learning is:
- Books
- Conferences
- Articles
- Discussions
- Other _____
- Videos
- Role playing
- YouTube
- Google

How am I going to achieve this learning?
Over the next _____ (1,2,3) _____ (days, weeks, months) I am committed to improving/learning:
_____
_____

What activities would further my learning objectives?
(Ex. Attend conferences, join a mastermind group, find or form a book club, explore chamber of commerce events, sign up for networking opportunities, commit to a philanthropic club).
_____
_____

Setbacks motivate me.
~ LINDSEY VONN

My top priorities today are:

1. _____

2. _____

3. _____

Today's challenges include:

1. _____

2. _____

3. _____

Leadership skills I need to remember / practice today:

1. _____

2. _____

3. _____

I can encourage others to succeed if I:

1. _____

2. _____

3. _____

Today's accomplishments:

_____
_____
_____

Overall, today was:
○ Rough
○ Meh
○ Okay
○ Good
○ Great

From today's challenges I learned:

_____
_____

I can make tomorrow even better if I:

_____

5-MINUTE LEADERSHIP PROMOTION PLAN

Part of being a great leader means fostering leadership in others. If people in your organization want to move into positions of greater responsibility, influence, and leadership, how do you support them? How do you know when they are ready, and what they want to do?

Ask the right questions!

Cultivating leaders starts with honest and open conversations. Ask!

1. Where do you see yourself in 3-5 years with us? What do you picture doing?
_____
_____
_____

2. What parts of this business/mission interest you?
_____
_____
_____

3. Where are you now in terms of your next position?
○ Totally ready now
○ Very well-prepared
○ Somewhat ready
○ Hopeful to start preparing

4. What current skills do you have that align well with your future desired position?
a. _____
b. _____
c. _____
d. _____
e. _____

5. What skills do you want to develop to be successful in your future roles?
a. _____
b. _____
c. _____
d. _____
e. _____

6. What is the plan of action to develop those critical skills?
a. _____
b. _____
c. _____
d. _____
e. _____

7. If you had two extra work hours per week to develop your skills, what would you do?
a. _____
b. _____
c. _____
d. _____
e. _____

To cultivate kindness is a valuable part of the business of life.
~ SAMUEL JOHNSON

My top priorities today are:

1. _____
2. _____
3. _____

Today's challenges include:

1. _____
2. _____
3. _____

Leadership skills I need to remember / practice today:

1. _____
2. _____
3. _____

I can encourage others to succeed if I:

1. _____
2. _____
3. _____

Today's accomplishments:

_____
_____
_____

Overall, today was:
○ Rough
○ Meh
○ Okay
○ Good
○ Great

From today's challenges I learned:
_____
_____

I can make tomorrow even better if I:
_____

5-MINUTE VOLUNTEER PLAN

People are motivated to donate time, energy, and resources because they have an emotional alignment with either the cause or the organization. People who volunteer generally start out extremely motivated. Over time, however, that sense of enthusiasm may wane, and the volunteer may eventually become burned out, discouraged, and resentful.

As leaders of organizations that rely on volunteers, we must treat our volunteers as well as we treat employees—offering meaningful work for them to do, not wasting their time, and making sure they feel like they're part of the team. Since they're not being paid, volunteers in general also need *more* appreciation and recognition.

Use these questions as guidelines to make sure you're treating your volunteers in a manner that supports retention and productivity!

When a volunteer shows up, do they know exactly what to do?

○ Yes ○ Maybe ○ No

Are the roles and responsibilities clearly defined?

○ Yes ○ Maybe ○ No

Do the volunteers know where to go for help if they get stuck?

○ Yes ○ Maybe ○ No

Are there written guidelines for the volunteers to follow?

○ Yes ○ Maybe ○ No

On a scale of 1-10, how would your volunteers rate your communication with them?

1 2 3 4 5 6 7 8 9 10
poor   good   fabulous

On a scale of 1-10, how would your volunteers rate you on how they feel their time is used?

1 2 3 4 5 6 7 8 9 10
time is wasted   mostly productive   very productive

Our volunteers could be even more productive if we provided training on:

1. _____
2. _____
3. _____

We know that volunteers who feel appreciated contribute more. On a scale of 1-10, would your volunteers say they feel?

1 2 3 4 5 6 7 8 9 10
mostly ignored   somewhat appreciated   very appreciated

We can better show appreciation to volunteers if we:

1. _____
2. _____
3. _____

Mistakes are the portals of discovery.
~ JAMES JOYCE

My top priorities today are:

1. _____
2. _____
3. _____

Today's challenges include:

1. _____
2. _____
3. _____

Leadership skills I need to remember / practice today:

1. _____
2. _____
3. _____

I can encourage others to succeed if I:

1. _____
2. _____
3. _____

Today's accomplishments:

_____
_____
_____

Overall, today was:
- ○ Rough
- ○ Meh
- ○ Okay
- ○ Good
- ○ Great

From today's challenges I learned:

_____
_____

I can make tomorrow even better if I:

_____

5-MINUTE WORK-LIFE BALANCE PLAN

Promoting work-life balance starts with leadership. Leaders need to recognize that employees need time away from work to re-energize, re-charge and re-focus. Many career-minded people are so focused on work that they work extra hours, don't use their vacation, and respond to emails on weekends.

People are our talent and top performers are in danger of burnout, chronic stress, and other associated health problems.

A good leader knows how to help people achieve an optimal work-life balance.

Workaholics need to be assured that their jobs are safe and that they need to take time off.

Overly relaxed workers need to be held accountable for deadlines.

Both can be helped by:

- Cooperatively setting realistic goals.
- Adjusting expectations for realistic performance.
- Allocating proper amounts of time for a project — not more and not less.

I can help people on our team budget time by:
1. _____
2. _____
3. _____

Leaders make it clear that taking vacation is expected.

To encourage people to take vacation:
- Leaders need to set the example by taking their own vacations.
- Provide work coverage for the person who is gone.
- Make time off a normal part of the work year.

Leaders honor their own stated work hours.

Many managers don't realize that their actions betray their words regarding work-life balance. They may say that working hours are 8 a.m.-4:30 p.m., but if they then show up at 7 a.m. and stay until 7 p.m, their teams receive a mixed message and may feel that they have to do the same.

Other ways leaders can help with work-life balance:

- Provide flexibility regarding what hours employees actually need to spend at work.

- Consider allowing remote work. This means employees are assessed on their outcomes instead of hours worked.

- Offer unique, healthy perks such as gym memberships and spa coupons.

- Be clear about expectations for answering work communications on nights and weekends.

I can promote a healthier work-life balance by:
1. _____
2. _____
3. _____
4. _____
5. _____
6. _____

SECTION 4

PERSONAL DEVELOPMENT

BETTER IN 52 WEEKS
ACTION STEPS TO A BETTER BUSINESS AND BETTER LIFE
with Less Stress and More Productivity

But just because it burns, doesn't mean you're gonna die.
You gotta get up and try, and try, and try.
~ PINK

My top priorities today are:

1. _____

2. _____

3. _____

Today's challenges include:

1. _____

2. _____

3. _____

Leadership skills I need to remember / practice today:

1. _____

2. _____

3. _____

I can encourage others to succeed if I:

1. _____

2. _____

3. _____

Today's accomplishments:

_____
_____
_____

Overall, today was:
○ Rough
○ Meh
○ Okay
○ Good
○ Great

From today's challenges I learned:

_____
_____

I can make tomorrow even better if I:

_____

5-MINUTE BUCKET LIST PLAN

What do we want to develop, improve, create, experience, achieve, influence or do? Are there places we want to visit? Thinking through and writing down the experiences and accomplishments that feel essential to a fulfilled, actualized life make them much more likely to happen. Studies show we're 42 percent more likely to achieve our goals if we write them down!

I'd like to learn...
_____
_____
_____
_____
_____

I'd like to travel to...
_____
_____
_____
_____
_____

and see the...
_____
_____
_____
_____
_____

I'd like to participate in a...
_____
_____
_____
_____
_____

I'd like to make sure I....
_____
_____
_____
_____
_____

I'd like to take...
_____
_____
_____
_____
_____

I'd like to give to...
_____
_____
_____
_____
_____

I'd like to pursue...
_____
_____
_____
_____
_____

I'd like to create...
_____
_____
_____
_____
_____

I'd like to leave a legacy of...
_____
_____
_____
_____
_____

Wherever you go, go with all your heart.
~ CONFUCIUS

My top priorities today are:

1. _____
_____
2. _____
_____
3. _____
_____

Today's challenges include:

1. _____
_____
2. _____
_____
3. _____
_____

Leadership skills I need to remember / practice today:

1. _____
_____
2. _____
_____
3. _____
_____

I can encourage others to succeed if I:

1. _____
_____
2. _____
_____
3. _____
_____

Today's accomplishments:

_____
_____
_____

Overall, today was:
○ Rough
○ Meh
○ Okay
○ Good
○ Great

From today's challenges I learned:

_____
_____

I can make tomorrow even better if I:

_____

5-MINUTE GRATITUDE PLAN

We know that people who reflect on gratitude are happier, feel valued, and experience fewer health issues. How can we live a more grateful life?

People who give to others, those who "pay it forward," show a greater neural sensitivity in the medial prefrontal cortex, the part of the brain associated with learning and decision-making.

- use positive emotional words
- use the word "we" more than "I"

Day _____
Date _____

On a scale of 1-10, today was _____

3 things that went well for me today:
1. _____
2. _____
3. _____

What did I accomplish today?
1. _____
2. _____
3. _____

What could have made today better?
1. _____
2. _____
3. _____

5 people I appreciated today:
1. _____
2. _____
3. _____

I worried about this today:
1. _____
2. _____
3. _____

I didn't need to worry about:
1. _____
2. _____
3. _____

*I don't wait for moods. You accomplish nothing if you do that.
Your mind must know it has got to get down to work.*

~ PEARL S. BUCK

My top priorities today are:

1. _____
   _____
2. _____
   _____
3. _____
   _____

Today's challenges include:

1. _____
   _____
2. _____
   _____
3. _____
   _____

Leadership skills I need to remember / practice today:

1. _____
   _____
2. _____
   _____
3. _____
   _____

I can encourage others to succeed if I:

1. _____
   _____
2. _____
   _____
3. _____
   _____

Today's accomplishments:

_____

_____

_____

Overall, today was:
○ Rough
○ Meh
○ Okay
○ Good
○ Great

From today's challenges I learned:

_____

_____

I can make tomorrow even better if I:

_____

5-MINUTE LIFE DOCUMENTS PLAN

Catastrophic events are challenging enough without the stress of trying to locate important information and instructions. Make it easier on yourself and your loved ones. Organize your important documents now so you and your family are prepared in the event of a natural disaster, emergency, or health care crisis.

Letters of Instruction
- **Child care form** (1 for each child)
- **Senior care form** (1 for each person)
- **Pet care form** (1 for each pet)

- **Will** - 1 for each person

- **Trust** - can be combined for a couple

- **Advisors** - (spiritual, financial, legal, medical, accounting, other)

- **Finances** - (bank, credit cards, investments, 401(k), SEP, IRA)

- **Retirement accounts** - (pensions, annuities, VA benefits, military retirement, Social Security payments)

- **Social Security death benefits**

- **Real estate** - (location, mortgage, rental and landlord information)

- **Military records** (DD-214)
- **Social Security card** (copy of)
- **Health care cards**

Insurance
- **Policy numbers, beneficiaries, location**
- **Life insurance**
- **Long-term health care**
- **Short-term disability**
- **Long-term disability**
- **House insurance**
- **Car insurance**
- **Boat insurance**
- **Umbrella insurance**

Vehicle Information
- **Car title**
- **Car loan**

- **Boat information**

- **Plane information** (hey, it could happen)

Utilities
- **Gas**
- **Electric**
- **Phone**
- **Cell phone**
- **Internet**
- **Water**
- **Trash**

Powers of Attorney - Durable
- **General**
- **Financial** (for each financial institution)

Health Care Directives
- **End of life care**
- **Do Not Resuscitate** (DNR), if applicable

Memorial Instructions/Preferences
- **Church/Synagogue/Mosque/Temple**
- **Service instructions** (readings, songs, pallbearers, eulogy, spiritual leader)

Funeral Arrangements
- **Prepaid plot**
- **Prepaid casket**
- **Cemetery**
- **Cremation versus burial**
- **Spiritual advisor**
- **Military honors**

Happiness lies in the joy of achievement and the thrill of creative effort.
~ FRANKLIN D. ROOSEVELT

My top priorities today are:

1. _____

2. _____

3. _____

Today's challenges include:

1. _____

2. _____

3. _____

Leadership skills I need to remember / practice today:

1. _____

2. _____

3. _____

I can encourage others to succeed if I:

1. _____

2. _____

3. _____

Today's accomplishments:

_____

_____

_____

Overall, today was:
- ○ Rough
- ○ Meh
- ○ Okay
- ○ Good
- ○ Great

From today's challenges I learned:

_____

_____

I can make tomorrow even better if I:

_____

5-MINUTE LIFE IMPROVEMENT PLAN

It is crucial that we take stock of the things, activities, and people that make our life more meaningful so that we can invest more time and energy into them. Determine what will truly improve your life and prioritize accordingly.

I take care of myself when I:
1. _____
2. _____
3. _____
4. _____
5. _____

To feel a sense of achievement I will devote time to:
1. _____
2. _____
3. _____
4. _____
5. _____

To improve my life, I will stop doing:
1. _____
2. _____
3. _____
4. _____
5. _____

I want to be known as someone who:
1. _____
2. _____
3. _____
4. _____
5. _____

I get the most stressed when I:
1. _____
2. _____
3. _____
4. _____
5. _____

I am happiest when I:
1. _____
2. _____
3. _____

I resolve to spend 1 minute every day for a total of 5 minutes per day, making my life better, by:
1. _____
2. _____
3. _____
4. _____
5. _____

The most important people in my life are:
1. _____
2. _____
3. _____
4. _____
5. _____

I spend time with my most important people when I:
1. _____
2. _____
3. _____
4. _____
5. _____

I show people I care when I:
1. _____
2. _____
3. _____
4. _____
5. _____

Champions keep playing until they get it right.
~ BILLIE JEAN KING

My top priorities today are:

1. _____
_____

2. _____
_____

3. _____
_____

Today's challenges include:

1. _____
_____

2. _____
_____

3. _____
_____

Leadership skills I need to remember / practice today:

1. _____
_____

2. _____
_____

3. _____
_____

I can encourage others to succeed if I:

1. _____
_____

2. _____
_____

3. _____
_____

Today's accomplishments:

_____
_____
_____

Overall, today was:
○ Rough
○ Meh
○ Okay
○ Good
○ Great

From today's challenges I learned:
_____
_____

I can make tomorrow even better if I:
_____

5-MINUTE MINDSET OPTIMIZATION PLAN

> A large part of personal and business success is determined by how and where we focus our thinking, efforts, and resources. What and whom we surround ourselves with, how we take care of ourselves, what we say, and where we put our attention matter. Take notice of how we think, where we invest our energy, and the environment we cultivate.

○ Yes	○ Maybe	○ No	I am successful in my occupation.
○ Yes	○ Maybe	○ No	My business focus can be even more successful.
○ Yes	○ Maybe	○ No	I surround myself with positive people.
○ Yes	○ Maybe	○ No	My closest friends do not complain a lot—they seem mostly happy.
○ Yes	○ Maybe	○ No	When I work, I feel energized.
○ Yes	○ Maybe	○ No	I have daily habits for success.
○ Yes	○ Maybe	○ No	I engage in healthy eating habits.
○ Yes	○ Maybe	○ No	I exercise or move my body regularly.
○ Yes	○ Maybe	○ No	I actively practice gratitude on a daily basis.
○ Yes	○ Maybe	○ No	I partner with others to increase success.
○ Yes	○ Maybe	○ No	I seek coaching/advice to guide my path towards greater achievement.
○ Yes	○ Maybe	○ No	I have a system in place to hold myself accountable.

People who answer "yes" to most of these questions tend to have more resilience and a solid support foundation. However, everyone can always improve!

The day you stop lookin' back is the day you start movin' on.
~ THOMAS RHETT

My top priorities today are:

1. _____

2. _____

3. _____

Today's challenges include:

1. _____

2. _____

3. _____

Leadership skills I need to remember / practice today:

1. _____

2. _____

3. _____

I can encourage others to succeed if I:

1. _____

2. _____

3. _____

Today's accomplishments:

_____
_____
_____

Overall, today was:
○ Rough
○ Meh
○ Okay
○ Good
○ Great

From today's challenges I learned:

_____
_____

I can make tomorrow even better if I:

_____

5-MINUTE MONEY PLAN

Without a plan, our money does not work for us. We work hard for a paycheck and it should work for us as well. Take a few minutes to create a financial plan.

Monthly Spending Plan/Budget

It's not what we make; it's what we don't spend.

I created a realistic spending plan on _____, _____(date). *(Free templates at http://productiveleaders.com/free-resources/free-stuff/)*

I resolve to save _____% of my income for retirement in a 401(k), IRA, or other retirement account.

I resolve to save $_____ for an emergency fund until I have $_____, which is 3-6 months of expenses.

I resolve to stop spending money on _____ _____ because it is not as important to me.

Retirement/Planning the Golden Years

Review retirement accounts to make sure they are aligned with retirement goals.

I can afford to retire at _____(age) if I save $_____ per month at a _____% rate of return.

Investments/Current Assets

These are non-retirement investments or other assets, including an emergency fund, a child's education fund, or non-specified savings and checking accounts.

True/False I understand the fees I am charged by my financial institutions.

True/False I understand my investments and know where they are.

True/False If I have one, I talk with my financial advisor at least twice a year.

Credit Cards/Plastic Budgeting

I manage my credit cards so that the bills are due on _____ of the month.

My APRs (Annual Percentage Rates) were reviewed on _____, _____ (date).

Real Estate/My Castle

My home's mortgage will be paid off on _____ (date) OR I am saving $_____/month for the down payment on a home.

If I add another $_____ more to the mortgage monthly payments I can have the loan paid off by _____, _____ (date).

Vacation/Planning for Fun

I am saving $_____/month for a vacation to _____ _____ where we will have fun seeing/visiting/traveling _____ _____ _____ _____ _____.

Leadership is action, not position.
~ DONALD H. MCGANNON

My top priorities today are:

1. _____
2. _____
3. _____

Today's challenges include:

1. _____
2. _____
3. _____

Leadership skills I need to remember / practice today:

1. _____
2. _____
3. _____

I can encourage others to succeed if I:

1. _____
2. _____
3. _____

Today's accomplishments:

_____
_____
_____

Overall, today was:
○ Rough
○ Meh
○ Okay
○ Good
○ Great

From today's challenges I learned:

_____
_____

I can make tomorrow even better if I:

_____

5-MINUTE VALUES PLAN

We only get one chance at this life, so let's make the most of it by doing what we were put here to do. Knowing what we're good at, understanding our strengths and challenges, and working steadily toward our goals keeps us from wasting days, weeks, or even years being distracted by things that don't matter. We don't have time to do everything, so we have to focus on what's most important and make choices that support our values.

It's important to understand what we value.

What's important to me? Examples might include: family, friends, dating, dog, cat, faith, career, money, sports, music, travel, or hobbies.

My top 5 priorities are:
1. _____
2. _____
3. _____
4. _____
5. _____

Many people are good at many things. What are you BEST at?

What am I naturally good at doing?
(If this question is difficult, ask friends what they see.)
1. _____
2. _____
3. _____
4. _____
5. _____

What are my top personality characteristics?

These are different from skills. These are adjectives friends would use to describe you—e.g. inquisitive, generous, energetic, friendly, passionate, kind, etc.
1. _____
2. _____
3. _____
4. _____
5. _____

What can I do to improve my skills?

Education, a degree, an internship, mentoring, coaching, job training?
1. _____
2. _____
3. _____
4. _____
5. _____

What is my life's purpose?
Try to answer "I am here to"...
_____
_____
_____
_____

What obstacles do I need to overcome or be aware of?
1. _____
2. _____
3. _____

What blogs, books, articles, periodicals help guide and motivate me?
_____
_____
_____
_____

Who are my trusted advisors? On whom can I call for help and advice?
_____
_____
_____
_____

What habits/behaviors can I try to eliminate in order to be more likeable?
_____
_____
_____
_____
_____

To be accountable for changing these behaviors I can:
1. _____
2. _____
3. _____
4. _____
5. _____

SECTION 5

PRODUCTIVITY

BETTER IN 52 WEEKS
ACTION STEPS TO A BETTER
BUSINESS AND BETTER LIFE
with Less Stress and More Productivity

Unhappiness is in not knowing what we want and killing ourselves to get it.

~ DON HEROLD

My top priorities today are:

1. _____
2. _____
3. _____

Today's challenges include:

1. _____
2. _____
3. _____

Leadership skills I need to remember / practice today:

1. _____
2. _____
3. _____

I can encourage others to succeed if I:

1. _____
2. _____
3. _____

Today's accomplishments:

_____
_____
_____

Overall, today was:
- ○ Rough
- ○ Meh
- ○ Okay
- ○ Good
- ○ Great

From today's challenges I learned:

_____
_____

I can make tomorrow even better if I:

_____

5-MINUTE EMAIL MANAGEMENT PLAN

One of the challenges of modern life, for leaders and employees, is managing the time and energy drain that our email inbox can be. Reading and responding can eat up vast amounts of valuable "deeper work" time. Used strategically, email is a useful tool. Used poorly, it creates overwhelm for ourselves and others. How do we deal with email in a productive and constructive way?

Triage email

Military people use 3 key strategies to help them organize and triage their email.

1. We use keywords in the subject line.
2. We include the deadlines.
3. We use the BLUF-Bottom Line Up Front.

Email has become a burden for most recipients today, so we want to make it easy for them to sort through their messages quickly—and find/respond to ours.

1. Keywords

Start every subject line with one of these keywords, based on Mary's acronym D.I.C.E.

- **Decide**
- **Information**
- **Coordinate**
- **Execute (Act)**

Example: If the recipient needs to take ACTION, start with Execute or Act, then describe the task.

2. Deadline

Part of this process means including the deadline in the subject line. The recipient should know by the first word what they have to do.

Example:
Subject: Act—Budget Submissions due Friday, August 30

3. BLUF

Then we use the BLUF—Bottom Line Up Front. This is the first sentence of the body of the email, and it quickly explains the Who, When, What, Where and Why.

EXAMPLE:
Budgets must be completed by Friday, August 30 and sent to the CFO's email, or else the budget defaults to zero for next year.

Then amplifying information follows.

This allows people to quickly sort their email by priority and deadlines.

Some corporate cultures do not appreciate such a direct approach, but others claim using D.I.C.E. and BLUF helps them:

- **regain lost time once spent searching through tasks with vague subject lines.**
- **find amplifying data on projects.**
- **plan their time.**
- **meet deadlines because everyone knows what is due when.**

For full description of Mary's email triage system, please visit **ProductiveLeaders.com/Triageemail**

Paralyze resistance with persistence.
~ WOODY HAYES

My top priorities today are:

1. _____
_____

2. _____
_____

3. _____
_____

Today's challenges include:

1. _____
_____

2. _____
_____

3. _____
_____

Leadership skills I need to remember / practice today:

1. _____
_____

2. _____
_____

3. _____
_____

I can encourage others to succeed if I:

1. _____
_____

2. _____
_____

3. _____
_____

Today's accomplishments:

_____
_____
_____

Overall, today was:
○ Rough
○ Meh
○ Okay
○ Good
○ Great

From today's challenges I learned:

_____
_____

I can make tomorrow even better if I:

_____

5-MINUTE FOCUS PLAN

Research claims that the average goldfish has an attention span of 9 seconds—and that humans today have an attention span of 8 seconds. Are goldfish able to focus better than we can? Is it because they don't have all of our distractions? Whatever the reason, focus is necessary to accomplish what we wish to. Fortunately, we can increase our attention spans and improve our ability to focus, both at home and at work.

Improve Your Ability To Focus
Start by eliminating distractions and training your brain to focus until the distractions stop being distractions.

Eliminate Distractions
SOUND is distracting to many people. Turn off sound notifications for texts, messages, emails, and phone calls. It may also include doorbells, radios, TVs, or anything else that causes focus to drift.

I resolve to turn off or schedule:
1. _____
2. _____
3. _____

LIGHTS or other visual movements distract some people, too. These people can increase their focus by working in places with minimal external stimuli.

PLACES to work best may include a library, an empty conference room, a quiet coffee shop, or off hours at a restaurant.

My best places to work include:
1. _____
2. _____
3. _____

Other distractions I need to eliminate:
1. _____
2. _____
3. _____

TIP: Some people are distracted by multiple tasks. Email is often a culprit. Stop checking emails several times per hour. Some people "batch" into your email accounts so that they only get emails a few times per day.

Staying Focused As A Goal
What is the most important task or job I can do today?
_____

What is the second most important task I can do today?
_____

For me to feel that today was a successful workday, I need to accomplish:
1. _____
2. _____
3. _____

TIP: If focusing is a problem, set a stopwatch or a computer timer for 1 minute and then focus completely on doing that job with full focus and attention.

Practice Focus
Focus becomes easier with practice.

What quick 1-minute jobs can I get out of the way NOW, so I can focus on what is really important:
1. _____
2. _____
3. _____

If you are always trying to be normal you will never know how amazing you can be.
~ MAYA ANGELOU

My top priorities today are:

1. _____
2. _____
3. _____

Today's challenges include:

1. _____
2. _____
3. _____

Leadership skills I need to remember / practice today:

1. _____
2. _____
3. _____

I can encourage others to succeed if I:

1. _____
2. _____
3. _____

Today's accomplishments:

_____
_____
_____

Overall, today was:
- ○ Rough
- ○ Meh
- ○ Okay
- ○ Good
- ○ Great

From today's challenges I learned:
_____
_____

I can make tomorrow even better if I:
_____

5-MINUTE OUTSOURCING PLAN

We all want to say "yes" to other people. We like feeling needed, and we enjoy the appreciation when we contribute. Some people hesitate to delegate because they think something won't be done the right way, or because it's simply quicker to do it themselves. Effective professionals know they have to triage their time, which can mean delegating or outsourcing jobs to others when it's appropriate.

When To Outsource

Consider delegating or outsourcing when:
1. The job is not something we are good at doing.
2. Someone else can do it at a lower opportunity cost. For example, if we make $30/hour and we can outsource a job for $10/hour, then outsourcing is a good option.
3. Another employee is trying to develop their skills and this job is an opportunity for them to gain visibility.
4. Someone wants to learn how to do that task.
5. It's someone else's job, but they have not been doing it correctly. Guide them and help them learn to do it properly.

Take Responsibility For Outsourcing

Many employees say their organizations will not pay for individual outsourcing. But if we can outsource tasks that others can do (often better than we can, and possibly more cheaply) and it gives us more time, this reduces stress and increases effectiveness.

Tasks To Consider Outsourcing

These are just a few common examples of tasks to save time, money and stress by outsourcing:

- **Phone calls**
- **Typing**
- **Research**
- **Data entry**
- **Video editing**
- **Creating spreadsheets**
- **Graphic design**
- **Presentation slides**
- **Web design**
- **Social media**
- **Prospecting**
- **Creating flyers**

If I outsourced these tasks, I'd save _____ hours per week.

Places To Find People To Outsource

- **Upwork**
- **Fiverr**
- **PeoplePerHour**
- **HireTheWorld**
- **Fancyhands**
- **Taskguru**
- **Independent virtual assistant**

_____
_____
_____

*The great leaders are like the best conductors—they reach beyond
the notes to reach the magic in the players.*

~ BLAINE LEE

My top priorities today are:

1. _____

2. _____

3. _____

Today's challenges include:

1. _____

2. _____

3. _____

Leadership skills I need to remember / practice today:

1. _____

2. _____

3. _____

I can encourage others to succeed if I:

1. _____

2. _____

3. _____

Today's accomplishments:

_____

_____

_____

Overall, today was:
○ Rough
○ Meh
○ Okay
○ Good
○ Great

From today's challenges I learned:

_____

_____

I can make tomorrow even better if I:

_____

5-MINUTE PRODUCTIVITY PLAN

Most people are not as productive as they could be because they waste time, do jobs inefficiently, or procrastinate on projects so that they fall behind and feel overwhelmed. Being productive means maximizing scarce resources, accomplishing what we want to accomplish, and spending time doing what we value.

Take Control

What are my top three outstanding projects right now? My life would be better if these projects were finished:

1. _____
2. _____
3. _____

Do I need help to get these done? ○ Yes   ○ No
Do I want help to get these done? ○ Yes   ○ No
If I had help, would they get done faster? ○ Yes   ○ No

Whom can I ask for help?
_____

SDS

To be more effective at the important things, stop doing the things that don't matter.
(SDS = Stop Doing Stupid)

What are three things I do on a daily basis that take up time that I do not need to do?

1. _____
2. _____
3. _____

Time Vampires

We all have people, events, and the unexpected crisis that take up our time. Sometimes other people impose their timelines into our lives and they waste our time, throwing us off schedule or not completing their part of a project that impact us.

Identify who or what wastes our time:

1. _____
2. _____
3. _____

Nice Ways To Stop Interruptions

I'm on deadline.
Can we please catch up later?
Thanks for stopping by. Good talking with you.

What works for me is:

1. _____
2. _____
3. _____

Do What We Do Best

We tend to gravitate toward those jobs that we like or are good at. ASK: "Am I the best person to do this? Can someone else do it better or at a lower opportunity cost?" If yes, consider outsourcing, or trade tasks with someone else.

I can outsource or trade:

1. _____
2. _____
3. _____

5-Minute Jobs

What can I get done today that will take less than 5 minutes? Return a call, walk the dog, do some pushups, send a card, post on social media, clear the desk, empty the trash, etc.

Quick tasks that will decrease my stress and increase my productivity:

1. _____
2. _____
3. _____

Nothing will work unless you do.
~ MAYA ANGELOU

My top priorities today are:

1. _____
2. _____
3. _____

Today's challenges include:

1. _____
2. _____
3. _____

Leadership skills I need to remember / practice today:

1. _____
2. _____
3. _____

I can encourage others to succeed if I:

1. _____
2. _____
3. _____

Today's accomplishments:

_____
_____
_____

Overall, today was:
○ Rough
○ Meh
○ Okay
○ Good
○ Great

From today's challenges I learned:

_____
_____

I can make tomorrow even better if I:

_____

5-MINUTE DAILY PRODUCTIVITY PLAN

DATE: _____

Calls to Make

Phone # or Person	Regarding

Appointments/Meetings

Time	Person/Place

Short-Term Goals

Follow Up

To Do

Today's Accomplishments

Just play. Have fun. Enjoy the game.
~ MICHAEL JORDAN

My top priorities today are:

1. _____
2. _____
3. _____

Today's challenges include:

1. _____
2. _____
3. _____

Leadership skills I need to remember / practice today:

1. _____
2. _____
3. _____

I can encourage others to succeed if I:

1. _____
2. _____
3. _____

Today's accomplishments:

_____
_____
_____

Overall, today was:
○ Rough
○ Meh
○ Okay
○ Good
○ Great

From today's challenges I learned:

_____
_____

I can make tomorrow even better if I:

_____

5-MINUTE PLAN-OF-THE-DAY PLAN

DAY: _____   **DATE:** _____

_____

Today's Focus

_____
_____
_____
_____

Reminders

1. _____
2. _____
3. _____

Errands

1. _____
2. _____
3. _____

Notes

_____
_____
_____
_____
_____

Appointments/Schedule

6:00a _____
7:00a _____
8:00a _____
9:00a _____
10:00a _____
11:00a _____
12:00p _____
1:00p _____
2:00p _____
3:00p _____
4:00p _____
5:00p _____
6:00p _____
7:00p _____
8:00p _____

He who will not risk cannot win.

~ JOHN PAUL JONES

My top priorities today are:

1. _____

2. _____

3. _____

Today's challenges include:

1. _____

2. _____

3. _____

Leadership skills I need to remember / practice today:

1. _____

2. _____

3. _____

I can encourage others to succeed if I:

1. _____

2. _____

3. _____

Today's accomplishments:

_____
_____
_____

Overall, today was:
○ Rough
○ Meh
○ Okay
○ Good
○ Great

From today's challenges I learned:

_____
_____

I can make tomorrow even better if I:

_____

5-MINUTE WEEKLY PRODUCTIVITY PLAN

WEEK STARTING: _____

☑	Action Plan	Time in Minutes	Due Date	Priority

SECTION 6

TEAMWORK

BETTER IN 52 WEEKS
ACTION STEPS TO A BETTER
BUSINESS AND BETTER LIFE
with Less Stress and More Productivity

*Always treat your employees exactly as
you want them to treat your best customers.*

~ STEPHEN R. COVEY

My top priorities today are:

1. _____
_____

2. _____
_____

3. _____
_____

Today's challenges include:

1. _____
_____

2. _____
_____

3. _____
_____

Leadership skills I need to remember / practice today:

1. _____
_____

2. _____
_____

3. _____
_____

I can encourage others to succeed if I:

1. _____
_____

2. _____
_____

3. _____
_____

Today's accomplishments:

_____
_____
_____

Overall, today was:
- ○ Rough
- ○ Meh
- ○ Okay
- ○ Good
- ○ Great

From today's challenges I learned:

_____
_____

I can make tomorrow even better if I:

_____

5-MINUTE APPRECIATION PLAN

People often struggle to feel valued and truly appreciated, both at home and at work. We all need to know that we matter. As managers and leaders, we want to create a place where employees love to come to work. Finding genuine ways to show appreciation is vital.

Our employees want us to hear their ideas, understand their perspectives, and help them overcome organizational obstacles. They also want to be appreciated.

When thanking people, show appreciation for a specific action in a way that resonates with the recipient and in a manner that doesn't come at the expense of others.

We discourage employee-of-the-month or employee-of-the-year programs because those recognition programs, which are intended to motivate people, instead often create competition and resentment among people who are supposed to be working together.

Here are some ways we can show appreciation to teammates and employees:

1. Send a thank-you note. In writing. By mail. **BONUS**: include a small gift card.

3. Send a thank-you email that is just to say thank you.

4. Thank the person who alerts us to a problem. We cannot fix something if we don't know about it.

5. Bring cookies. Or brownies. Or donuts. Or energy bars. Or anything that is easily shared with others to the office.

6. Thank people publicly in an online forum.

7. Take a picture of a person and turn it into a thank-you card.

8. Make a personalized video to say thank you.

9. Create a thank-you white board or bulletin board, where people can publicly thank others for specific actions.

10. Send an article that would be helpful, or about something of interest to someone. Say "I thought of you!"

11. Make a donation to that person's favorite charity.

12. Schedule lunch to be delivered.

13. Buy a handful of $10 gift cards and make it a goal to give them out to teammates who are doing something nice for others.

14. Schedule bring-your-dog-to-work day. Allow people with allergies to work from home that day.

15. Schedule "productivity days" where employees can choose to work from home.

16. Schedule a massage therapist to come to the office and give people neck massages.

17. Encourage volunteer or self-care afternoons, where people are encouraged to get away from the office and do something fun and different.

18. Offer tickets to a play, concert, or sports event.

19. Take a meeting outside to a park and have a picnic.

20. Have a thought-of-the-week whiteboard. Encourage anonymous comments by asking interesting questions such as:
With whom in history would you like to have dinne? What was your first job? Where would you go on a dream vacation? What is your favorite Christmas cookie?

First we form habits, then they form us.
Conquer your bad habits, or they'll eventually conquer you.

~ ROB GILBERT

My top priorities today are:

1. _____
2. _____
3. _____

Today's challenges include:

1. _____
2. _____
3. _____

Leadership skills I need to remember / practice today:

1. _____
2. _____
3. _____

I can encourage others to succeed if I:

1. _____
2. _____
3. _____

Today's accomplishments:

_____
_____
_____

Overall, today was:
○ Rough
○ Meh
○ Okay
○ Good
○ Great

From today's challenges I learned:
_____
_____

I can make tomorrow even better if I:
_____

5-MINUTE EMPLOYEE ENGAGEMENT PLAN

Less than 33% of Americans are considered "engaged" in their jobs. Engaged employees are enthusiastic and excited about their work, and happy in their current environment. Disengaged employees are not concerned about organizational vision, goals, or their own performance. As a result, organizational growth and outcomes are delayed, there is less creativity, and morale decreases.

What can leaders do to facilitate engagement at work?

Leaders can provide clear communication and honest feedback to make sure employees understand their roles in the organization.

We help achieve our goals because we provide:
_____
_____
_____
_____

We rely on our people for:
_____
_____
_____
_____

Leaders also keep employees motivated and challenged at work.

Ask questions such as:

What particular strengths do you want to utilize more?
1. _____
2. _____
3. _____

Are there any specific projects we're doing here that you would like to be involved in?
1. _____
2. _____
3. _____

Do you want more responsibility? With what?
1. _____
2. _____
3. _____

Do you want less responsibility? What would you prefer not doing?
1. _____
2. _____
3. _____

Leaders make sure their employees have the training they need to do their jobs well.

Leaders find out what employees want to further their careers and job skills by asking:

1. What would you like more training on?
2. What would you like to learn next?
3. Is there anyone here you'd like to learn from?

Leaders strive to improve the workplace for their people.

1. What can we do to make the workplace more enjoyable for you?
2. If you were your own boss, what would you change?
3. Are we challenging you enough?
4. Are there any tools or technology that would help you do your job better?

Leaders provide positive feedback quickly.
What gets rewarded gets repeated.

"I've noticed you're great at
_____."
"You handled that difficult customer really well."
"_____ is one of your strengths and I am impressed with how you _____."

The more you praise and celebrate your life, the more there is in life to celebrate.
~ OPRAH WINFREY

My top priorities today are:

1. _____
2. _____
3. _____

Today's challenges include:

1. _____
2. _____
3. _____

Leadership skills I need to remember / practice today:

1. _____
2. _____
3. _____

I can encourage others to succeed if I:

1. _____
2. _____
3. _____

Today's accomplishments:

_____
_____
_____

Overall, today was:
○ Rough
○ Meh
○ Okay
○ Good
○ Great

From today's challenges I learned:

_____
_____

I can make tomorrow even better if I:

_____

5-MINUTE EMPLOYEE MORALE PLAN

Keeping employees motivated and happy at work is crucial to maintaining productivity. Good morale comes from a workplace that is supportive, encouraging, and focused on the employee. Managers and leaders can help people be successful by frequently checking in, offering assistance, and showing interest in employees' development. 67% of millennials say they would leave an organization that was uninterested in their professional development.

To increase morale, start by checking in, showing care, and asking the right questions. Ask:

What keeps you motivated at work?
- ____ My supervisor
- ____ Flexibility
- ____ Problem-solving
- ____ My team members
- ____ Challenges
- ____ The actual work
- ____ Making a difference
- ____ Customers
- ____ The organization's mission
- ____ The workspace/environment
- ____ I just wake up motivated

Leaders can renew motivation by asking:

1. Name something you do at work that you really enjoy?
_____
_____
_____

2. What do you like best about this work space?
_____
_____
_____

3. What would make our work space more enjoyable or comfortable?
_____
_____
_____

4. How can we help you develop or reach your full potential?
_____
_____
_____

5. What needs do you have that are not met by the job or the work space?
_____
_____
_____

6. What is your favorite thing about this job or this organization?
_____
_____
_____

7. What most needs improvement in this organization?
_____
_____
_____

Defeat is not the worst of failures. Not to have tried is the true failure.
~ GEORGE E. WOODBERRY

My top priorities today are:

1. _____
   _____
2. _____
   _____
3. _____
   _____

Today's challenges include:

1. _____
   _____
2. _____
   _____
3. _____
   _____

Leadership skills I need to remember / practice today:

1. _____
   _____
2. _____
   _____
3. _____
   _____

I can encourage others to succeed if I:

1. _____
   _____
2. _____
   _____
3. _____
   _____

Today's accomplishments:

_____
_____
_____

Overall, today was:
○ Rough
○ Meh
○ Okay
○ Good
○ Great

From today's challenges I learned:

_____
_____

I can make tomorrow even better if I:

_____

5-MINUTE EMPLOYEE RELATIONSHIP PLAN

Even the best-performing organizations struggle with keeping and building healthy interactions between people at work. Making assumptions, believing that others share your opinion, and waiting to move forward on a project when others may not be totally committed can damage work relationships.

Help people work harmoniously together by understanding:

1. Not everyone shares your opinions and they shouldn't.

a. I will get more ideas if I _____
_____
_____

b. I can help people express their ideas when I _____
_____
_____
_____

c. I can encourage people around me to discuss their opinions when I use phrases like:
_____
_____
_____

2. People respond to incentives. Incentives can be:

   a. Salary
   b. Bonuses
   c. Flexibility
   d. Benefits
   e. Perks—concert tickets, sports tickets, restaurant/gift cards
   f. New projects
   g. Travel
   h. Access to senior people

I prefer _____ incentives.

I can motivate others with these incentives:
_____
_____
_____

3. The "niceties" are nice at work.

It's easy to be rushed, feel frantic, and neglect some of the politeness at work. We need to remember those magic words we were taught as children. We need to be more polite at work.

   a. Say please and thank you
   b. Acknowledge people who are being helpful
   c. Use language with your people that you use with clients
   d. Look at people when they talk with you
   e. I can be more polite at work when I
_____
_____

4. The boss is held to a higher standard.

While employees appreciate a leader who is approachable for conversation, and one who is willing to pitch in, leaders need to realize that employees watch their leader's actions carefully. Leaders must set the example for others to follow.

What can I do at work to set an even better example?
_____
_____

5. People respond differently to change.

People who like change say it invigorates them and helps them be more creative and productive. People who prefer the status quo often respond to change with denial or by ignoring the new shifts. People are different, and they need different techniques to help them deal with risk or change at work.

People who like risk need: _____
_____

People who prefer status quo need: _____
_____

He that won't be counseled can't be helped.
~ BENJAMIN FRANKLIN

My top priorities today are:

1. _____

2. _____

3. _____

Today's challenges include:

1. _____

2. _____

3. _____

Leadership skills I need to remember / practice today:

1. _____

2. _____

3. _____

I can encourage others to succeed if I:

1. _____

2. _____

3. _____

Today's accomplishments:

_____
_____
_____

Overall, today was:
○ Rough
○ Meh
○ Okay
○ Good
○ Great

From today's challenges I learned:
_____
_____

I can make tomorrow even better if I:
_____

5-MINUTE KNOW YOUR PEOPLE PLAN

In order to foster high-performing, engaged teams, leaders need to know their team members. Use this plan to take inventory of your team members' motivations, preferences, and goals.

Managers and leaders need to ask questions that help them understand their team, and communicate with people in a way that makes them feel seen, known and cared about.

Leaders need to know who their people are, what motivates them, what they're worried about, and what they need from their leadership.

1. What is your DISC profile? (DISC is a behavior/personal assessment tool.)
_____
_____

2. What is your Myers-Briggs description?
_____
_____

3. How long have you been with us?
_____ yrs _____ months

4. How long have you served in this position?
_____ yrs _____ months

5. What do you like best about your job?
_____
_____

6. What would you like to do MORE of?
_____
_____

7. What would you like to do LESS of?
_____
_____

8. What are your top 3 goals in this job this year?
_____
_____
_____

9. What did you worry about last year that you don't have to worry about this year?
_____
_____

10. What are your top concerns now?
_____
_____

11. What do you need from me to help you achieve your goals?
_____
_____

Unless you try to do something beyond what you have already mastered, you will never grow.

~ RONALD E. OSBORN

My top priorities today are:

1. _____

2. _____

3. _____

Today's challenges include:

1. _____

2. _____

3. _____

Leadership skills I need to remember / practice today:

1. _____

2. _____

3. _____

I can encourage others to succeed if I:

1. _____

2. _____

3. _____

Today's accomplishments:

_____

_____

_____

Overall, today was:
- ○ Rough
- ○ Meh
- ○ Okay
- ○ Good
- ○ Great

From today's challenges I learned:

_____

_____

I can make tomorrow even better if I:

_____

5-MINUTE LIKABILITY PLAN

Can we become more likeable? Yes! That doesn't mean being someone we're not—it means projecting who we are in a way that relates well to others. People who are likeable appear to genuinely care about other people. They remember details and show interest in their lives.

People who are likeable often exhibit traits like:

1. _____
2. _____
3. _____
4. _____
5. _____

People enjoy being around people who show an interest in them.

We can show other people that we are interested in them by being better at:

1. _____
2. _____
3. _____
4. _____
5. _____

People who are likeable often compliment other people.

Think of all of the people we are around every day. Try this exercise. Genuinely compliment 5 people today. Co-workers, wait staff, strangers in a grocery store, cashiers, and people at your child's school—all might benefit from a genuine compliment.

PERSON	COMPLIMENTED FOR
1. _____	_____
2. _____	_____
3. _____	_____
4. _____	_____
5. _____	_____

Being likeable also means NOT doing some actions that might be considered offensive or rude.

What things do other people do that you find irritating? (This is usually the easiest part of this plan.)

1. _____
2. _____
3. _____
4. _____
5. _____

What habits/behaviors can I try to eliminate in order to be more likeable?

I RESOLVE TO STOP:

1. _____
2. _____
3. _____
4. _____
5. _____

To be accountable for changing these behaviors I can:

1. _____
2. _____
3. _____
4. _____
5. _____

Writing is thinking on paper.
~ WILLIAM ZINSSER

My top priorities today are:

1. _____

2. _____

3. _____

Today's challenges include:

1. _____

2. _____

3. _____

Leadership skills I need to remember / practice today:

1. _____

2. _____

3. _____

I can encourage others to succeed if I:

1. _____

2. _____

3. _____

Today's accomplishments:

_____
_____
_____

Overall, today was:
○ Rough
○ Meh
○ Okay
○ Good
○ Great

From today's challenges I learned:
_____
_____

I can make tomorrow even better if I:
_____

5-MINUTE MEETINGS PLAN

Even though meetings are still one of the most effective ways for people to share ideas, exchange information, collaborate, and make decisions, most workers complain that meetings are a waste of time. Leaders need to make sure their meetings are effective and generating results.

Planning meetings

Before you call a meeting, ask:
- Is this meeting necessary?
- Can I get the same information and the same buy-in from an email discussion?
- Have I given people enough time to properly prepare and clear their calendar to attend?
- Is this the best use of my time?
- Is this the best use of my employee's time?

When planning the meeting, ask:

1. What is the purpose of this meeting? Are we here to:
- Share information?
- Make decisions?
- Brainstorm for new ideas?
- Coalesce team members around a central idea?
- Obtain updates from various departments?

2. What do we need to achieve/accomplish in this meeting?
_____
_____
_____
_____

3. Who needs to be at the meeting?
Are there some people who are vital, meaning that we cannot move forward with the meeting without them? Are they available?

Person	Role	Critical? Y/N
_____	_____	_____
_____	_____	_____
_____	_____	_____

Create an agenda

Once the goals, the participants, and the outcomes are clear, create an agenda for the meeting.

Every meeting needs and agenda. The agenda should be promulgated to every attendee 24 hours in advance. This shows that managers are not wasting their team's time.

The meeting agenda should include:

1. The meeting's focus
2. The beginning and ending time
3. What participants need to prepare or bring
4. A list of discussion topics
5. The time allotted for each discussion topic
6. The person responsible for the discussion topic

Meeting tips

1. Start on time. If we wait while people drift in, people will learn that showing up on time wastes more of their time so they will also start showing up late.
2. End on time to show respect for people's time.
3. Make sure everyone gets a chance to be heard.
4. If we are in charge, wait to provide an opinion until last to make sure people don't feel that they have to agree with leadership.

If you don't know where you are going, any road will get you there.
~ LEWIS CARROLL

My top priorities today are:

1. _____
_____

2. _____
_____

3. _____
_____

Today's challenges include:

1. _____
_____

2. _____
_____

3. _____
_____

Leadership skills I need to remember / practice today:

1. _____
_____

2. _____
_____

3. _____
_____

I can encourage others to succeed if I:

1. _____
_____

2. _____
_____

3. _____
_____

Today's accomplishments:

_____
_____
_____

Overall, today was:
○ Rough
○ Meh
○ Okay
○ Good
○ Great

From today's challenges I learned:

_____
_____

I can make tomorrow even better if I:

_____

5-MINUTE MOTIVATION PLAN

Let's face it: some days are better than others. We know that if we don't take action to get tasks accomplished right away, we risk not getting them done at all. But some days we just don't feel like doing what we need to do. How do we pick ourselves up when intrinsic motivation is running low? How do we regain our normal levels of focus, energy, and drive?

Here are some quick activities or exercises that we can engage in to regain some momentum when we're feeling unmotivated.

Overcoming procrastination

We often feel unmotivated because we feel overwhelmed with everything we have to do. Getting our priorities organized and getting parts of a project completed help move us forward.

Sometimes getting started on a job we don't want to do is the hardest part. If we have procrastinated on a project, even starting to work on it seems overwhelming.

Try these strategies:

- Set a timer and work for 5 minutes on a project you hate
- Get a friend or a co-worker to help you break through the part of the task that is holding you back
- Hire someone who will work with you on a project that seems daunting

Be surrounded by motivation

Other people affect our mood and motivation. When possible, we need to surround ourselves with people who are motivated and productive. When others start to draw us into negative, whining conversation, we can focus on what is motivating and positive by helping others be more positive.

Ask questions that help others refocus:
- "What has gone well for you today?"
- "What are you really proud of right now?"
- "What project have you completed?"
- "What is the silver lining here?"
- "What were you worried about yesterday that you don't need to worry about today?"
- "Can you summarize everything good that happened in this situation?"

Revisit the purpose

Trying to do something for the sake of doing it often isn't very motivating. When we've broken a task down into pieces, we can lose sight of the whole. We need to widen the lens, look at the big picture and connect what we're doing with WHY we're doing it. The deeper, stronger and bigger the "why," the more compelling our motivation.

Try asking:
What will this task/project allow me/us to do?
Why is this work important?
How will this make a difference?
Whom and what does this support?
This task matters because _____
_____.

The journey of a thousand miles begins with one step.
~ LAO TZU

My top priorities today are:

1. _____
2. _____
3. _____

Today's challenges include:

1. _____
2. _____
3. _____

Leadership skills I need to remember / practice today:

1. _____
2. _____
3. _____

I can encourage others to succeed if I:

1. _____
2. _____
3. _____

Today's accomplishments:

_____
_____
_____

Overall, today was:
○ Rough
○ Meh
○ Okay
○ Good
○ Great

From today's challenges I learned:

_____
_____

I can make tomorrow even better if I:

_____

5-MINUTE TEAM BUILDING PLAN

Building a strong team means having the right team dynamics, as well as the right team members. Collective intelligence studies show that highly functioning teams increase overall combined intelligence and improve results. We are truly better together.

What do great teams need?

1. **Clearly articulated vision**
2. **Understandable mission**
3. **Corporate culture/attitude of success**
4. **Adaptability/willingness to change**

Work with the goal in mind.

What builds teamwork in my workplace?
1. _____
2. _____
3. _____
4. _____

What is working well in my workplace?
1. _____
2. _____
3. _____
4. _____

What destroys teams?
1. _____
2. _____
3. _____
4. _____

What can I stop doing that may be harming the team?
1. _____
2. _____
3. _____
4. _____

Team players

Some people just seem to be naturally good at being team players. Why? What makes great team players so valuable to an organization?
1. _____
2. _____
3. _____
4. _____

What do great team players do that makes everyone want to work with them?
1. _____
2. _____
3. _____
4. _____

What can I do to cultivate those qualities in myself?
1. _____
2. _____
3. _____
4. _____

What are some characteristics the rest of the team or workplace expects from me?
1. _____
2. _____
3. _____
4. _____

Never interrupt your enemy when he is making a mistake.
~ NAPOLEON BONAPARTE

My top priorities today are:

1. _____
2. _____
3. _____

Today's challenges include:

1. _____
2. _____
3. _____

Leadership skills I need to remember / practice today:

1. _____
2. _____
3. _____

I can encourage others to succeed if I:

1. _____
2. _____
3. _____

Today's accomplishments:

_____
_____
_____

Overall, today was:
○ Rough
○ Meh
○ Okay
○ Good
○ Great

From today's challenges I learned:

_____
_____

I can make tomorrow even better if I:

_____

5-MINUTE TRUST PLAN

Trust is assumed until it's lost, and it can be easy to lose. Many leaders and managers inadvertently lose trust, and then wonder why the people around them are not being productive, communicative, and forthcoming.

If you want people to trust you, be trustworthy.

Keep people informed, keep their perspective in mind, and keep your promises.

Here are some ways trust is lost, and how we can rebuild it.

Ways To Lose Trust

- Hoard information
- Hide processes
- Speak disrespectfully
- Create uncertainty
- Be vague about the employee's roles + career
- Lie
- Steal company time
- Misappropriate resources
- Make poor decisions
- Apply rules unfairly
- Set unattainable goals
- Gossip about others
- Don't accept responsibility
- Pit people against each other
- Be quick to place blame on others
- Promise, but don't deliver

Ways To Build Trust

- Share information
- Be transparent
- Treat everyone like your best client
- Provide information people need
- Consistently mentor employees
- Be truthful
- Let people know where you are
- Be careful about how actions are perceived
- Gather data + listen before making decisions
- Create compelling and possible milestones
- Be kind when talking about others
- Encourage cooperation
- Fix the problem, not the blame
- Underpromise and overdeliver

In my organization, I can build trust when I:

_____
_____
_____
_____
_____
_____
_____
_____
_____

BONUS SECTION

SUPER ACHIEVERS

BETTER IN 52 WEEKS
ACTION STEPS TO A BETTER BUSINESS AND BETTER LIFE
with Less Stress and More Productivity

I'd rather regret the things I've done than regret the things I haven't done.
~ LUCILLE BALL

My top priorities today are:

1. _____

2. _____

3. _____

Today's challenges include:

1. _____

2. _____

3. _____

Leadership skills I need to remember / practice today:

1. _____

2. _____

3. _____

I can encourage others to succeed if I:

1. _____

2. _____

3. _____

Today's accomplishments:

_____
_____
_____

Overall, today was:
- ○ Rough
- ○ Meh
- ○ Okay
- ○ Good
- ○ Great

From today's challenges I learned:
_____
_____

I can make tomorrow even better if I:
_____

5-MINUTE "WHAT IF?" CRISIS PLAN

We often worry about things that might not happen. Part of great leadership means planning for the worst possible situations, and then working backwards. This means creating contingency plans for all kinds of variables, and then realistically planning for different scenarios.

The best leaders hope for the best, plan for the worst, and are realistic. They help their people adapt, and lead them to quickly and calmly move to a contingency plan.

To start the "what if?" crisis planning process, leaders need to ask:

1. What is the worst case scenario?
_____
_____
_____

What is our plan to handle that worst-case scenario?
_____
_____
_____

What specific actions do we need to implement if this worst-case scenario happens?
_____
_____
_____

2. What is the best-case scenario?
_____
_____
_____

Remember, being calm in a crisis is contagious. Being calm inspires confidence. Staying calm throughout an emergency increases trust.

What is our plan to handle that best-case scenario?
_____
_____
_____

What specific actions do we need to implement if this best-case scenario happens?
_____
_____
_____

3. What is the most likely scenario?
_____
_____
_____

What is our plan to handle the most likely scenario?
_____
_____
_____

What specific actions will we need to implement if this most likely scenario happens?
_____
_____
_____

Let your dreams stay big and your worries stay small.
~ RASCAL FLATTS

My top priorities today are:

1. _____

2. _____

3. _____

Today's challenges include:

1. _____

2. _____

3. _____

Leadership skills I need to remember / practice today:

1. _____

2. _____

3. _____

I can encourage others to succeed if I:

1. _____

2. _____

3. _____

Today's accomplishments:

_____

_____

_____

Overall, today was:
- ○ Rough
- ○ Meh
- ○ Okay
- ○ Good
- ○ Great

From today's challenges I learned:

_____

_____

I can make tomorrow even better if I:

_____

5-MINUTE OPPORTUNITY PLAN

In the middle of fast-paced changes and a fluctuating environment, it is easy to freeze into inactivity. During times of turmoil and disruption is when people need their leaders the most. This is also the time to find opportunities.

Humans do not like change. We prefer security and stability, which is why change, for most people, is difficult. The habenula, that part of our brain which helps us deal with change, doesn't like it. Once we accept the change, we tend to adapt fairly quickly.

For some people, it is tough to see opportunities when situations are changing, especially if they are changing due to events outside of our control. Great leaders are not only resilient during adversity, they also synthesize information quickly, and then take the right action fast. They are able to see opportunities even in tough situations.

Every challenge brings with it the opportunity to help others, solve problems, and move forward. As leaders, that is why we are here.

It is helpful to ask questions such as:

Where are there unmet needs where we can help?
_____
_____

Where can I best serve other people?
_____
_____

Where can I best serve my team?
_____
_____

Where can we best serve our clients, customers, patients, and members?
_____
_____

What are my people's immediate needs right now?
_____
_____

If I had plenty of money, resources, and time, what would I do first?
_____
_____

What needs to be invented to solve this problem?
_____
_____

What is the craziest possible idea for this situation?
_____
_____

What is the craziest impossible idea for this situation?
_____
_____

What needs to be invented or developed for the impossible solution to work?
_____
_____

What are the benefits of having this challenge right now?
_____
_____

In a year, what will we say was a great outcome of this situation?
_____
_____

*Limitations live only in our minds. But if we use our imaginations,
our possibilities become limitless.*

~ JAMIE PAOLINETTI

My top priorities today are:

1. _____
   _____
2. _____
   _____
3. _____
   _____

Today's challenges include:

1. _____
   _____
2. _____
   _____
3. _____
   _____

Leadership skills I need to remember / practice today:

1. _____
   _____
2. _____
   _____
3. _____
   _____

I can encourage others to succeed if I:

1. _____
   _____
2. _____
   _____
3. _____
   _____

Today's accomplishments:

_____
_____
_____

Overall, today was:
- ○ Rough
- ○ Meh
- ○ Okay
- ○ Good
- ○ Great

From today's challenges I learned:

_____
_____

I can make tomorrow even better if I:

_____

5-MINUTE P.I.V.O.T. PLAN

Resilient leaders help people adapt quickly during times of crisis and change. They pivot. They take the right action at the right time.

Using P.I.V.O.T. as an acronym, this exercise helps people focus on what is most important, and identifies specific actions to take to move forward.

P=Purpose. What is important to you? What drives you? What gives you meaning?

Circle 3 words that describe your purpose—what you most want to do.

prosper	progress	promote	propel	propose
possess	prompt	pacify	prepare	perfect
produce	participate	perceive	persist	persuade
plan	pledge	praise	present	proceed
prevent	promise	provide	publish	

I=Inspire.

Circle 3 words that inspire you when you think of your life's work:

ignite	imagine	imbue	immerse	impart
impress	improve	include	incorporate	increase
inform	influence	invest	innovate	instill

Answer the following questions using three of the i-words words you circled above:

EX: This is a great time for me to <u>ignite</u> my promise to spend more time with my friends.
EX: This is a great time for me to <u>impart</u> my knowledge to others through more mentorship.
EX: This is a great time for me to <u>innovate</u> my business with new products and services.

1. This is a great time for me to i_____ my _____ to _____ by _____.

2. This is a great time for me to i_____ my _____ to _____ through _____.

3. This is a great time for me to i_____ my _____ with/for _____.

V=Volatility. Every major shift comes with a degree of uncertainty. Where are you right now on this spectrum? Where is your team?

Circle the word or area that best describes how you feel about the changing environment:

vague - - - vexed - - - volatile - - - valuable - - - victorious

O=Opportunities. What specific opportunities do you see right now? Where is there a need in your community? In your industry? In your business?

1. _____
2. _____
3. _____
4. _____
5. _____

T= Tools/Training/Technology. What additional tools, training or technology do you need that would make you more successful?

Tools:
Get a new _____
Use an app to _____
Learn how to use _____

Training/Development:
Take a course in _____
Contact _____ for advice
Read _____

Technology
Do I need to invent it? _____
What can be automated? _____
What can be simplified? _____

The universe is change; our life is what our thoughts make it.
~ MARCUS AURELIUS

My top priorities today are:

1. _____
   _____
2. _____
   _____
3. _____
   _____

Today's challenges include:

1. _____
   _____
2. _____
   _____
3. _____
   _____

Leadership skills I need to remember / practice today:

1. _____
   _____
2. _____
   _____
3. _____
   _____

I can encourage others to succeed if I:

1. _____
   _____
2. _____
   _____
3. _____
   _____

Today's accomplishments:

_____
_____
_____

Overall, today was:
- ○ Rough
- ○ Meh
- ○ Okay
- ○ Good
- ○ Great

From today's challenges I learned:
_____
_____

I can make tomorrow even better if I:
_____

5-MINUTE PROBLEM-SOLVING PLAN

Discerning the true nature of an actual problem is a challenge. Leaders need to consider all possible courses of action, and the consequences of each action, both intentional and unintentional. We have all known people who rush into a situation and the unintended consequences are worse than the original problem. Part of the leader's job is to discover the true nature of a problem so that they can make the best possible decision, at that time, with the information available.

Leaders need to ask questions, such as:

How did this problem start?
_____
_____

How long has this situation been going on?
_____
_____

When did this problem get to this level?
_____
_____

What is the background of this problem?
_____
_____

Are there any personalities involved that have prevented us from solving this problem in the past?
_____
_____

What do you think is the single most important thing I need to know to make a good decision? *(ask several people this question)*
_____
_____

Is waiting for more information a better or a worse option?
_____
_____

What are the unintended consequences we need to consider?
_____
_____

What is the simplest and cheapest solution in the short run?
_____
_____

What is the simplest and cheapest solution in the long run?
_____
_____

What is the most complicated and expensive solution in the short run?
_____
_____

What is the most complicated and expensive solution in the long run?
_____
_____

What action should we take right now?
1. _____
2. _____
3. _____
4. _____
5. _____
6. _____

It is literally true that you can succeed best and quickest by helping others to succeed.
~NAPOLEON HILL

My top priorities today are:

1. _____

2. _____

3. _____

Today's challenges include:

1. _____

2. _____

3. _____

Leadership skills I need to remember / practice today:

1. _____

2. _____

3. _____

I can encourage others to succeed if I:

1. _____

2. _____

3. _____

Today's accomplishments:

_____
_____
_____

Overall, today was:
○ Rough
○ Meh
○ Okay
○ Good
○ Great

From today's challenges I learned:

_____
_____

I can make tomorrow even better if I:

_____

5-MINUTE EXECUTIVE COACHING PLAN

We believe that everyone can be an even better leader, manager, and mentor. Just like a professional athlete, having coach or advisor helps us all become better. We can talk through ideas, brainstorm, and discuss the best ways to solve problems.

The coach or advisor provides helpful feedback, acts as a sounding board, and gives guidance on directives when appropriate. To help others, we provide this checklist we find effective when thinking about establishing a coaching program.

When pairing a coach with a leader, we ask:
- What would be a good result or outcome?
- How will we measure success?
- Is the coach a good personality fit for this leader?
- Is there mutual respect between the advisor and the organization?
- Does the executive coach or advisor understand the business and the business model?
- Is there an understanding of that organization's desired result?
- What kind of confidentiality is involved?

During the first meeting between the coach and leader:
- Identify the purpose of the coaching
- Identify the frequency and the means of communication
- Be clear on the tools used to measure and acheive results
- Share commonalities that create trust
- Address uncertainties
- Reiterate the vision, mission, and goals

Throughout the process:
- Maintain frequent communication, even if it is short phone calls, texts, or emails
- Set and revise the agenda for long-term results
- Have honest dialogues
- Identify behaviors that may need altering with positive action steps
- Continuously assess current issues and business challenges

For me to work with a coach or executive advisor I need:
Someone who is _____
will push me to _____
and helps me to work through _____

Happiness is not by chance, but by choice.
~JIM ROHN

My top priorities today are:

1. _____
   _____
2. _____
   _____
3. _____
   _____

Today's challenges include:

1. _____
   _____
2. _____
   _____
3. _____
   _____

Leadership skills I need to remember / practice today:

1. _____
   _____
2. _____
   _____
3. _____
   _____

I can encourage others to succeed if I:

1. _____
   _____
2. _____
   _____
3. _____
   _____

Today's accomplishments:

_____
_____
_____

Overall, today was:
- ○ Rough
- ○ Meh
- ○ Okay
- ○ Good
- ○ Great

From today's challenges I learned:

_____
_____

I can make tomorrow even better if I:

_____

5-MINUTE COACHING PLAN

Many leaders are called upon to mentor and coach their employees. Rising leaders want and need guidance from experienced executives. Sometimes it is difficult to start the conversation. These questions are designed to prompt dialogue about what is needed to develop the skills, abilities, and experience to move others toward full potential.

Define Personal Success:

Think about your perfect future life. What do you see?
_____

Where, geographically, do you want to live?
_____

What factors do you need to have a happy personal life?
1. _____
2. _____
3. _____

What are your most important relationships? Name them.
Family: _____
Friends: _____
Work: _____
Community: _____

What do you want to be known for on a personal level?
1. _____
2. _____
3. _____

Develop Professionally:

What got you into this work?
_____

What unique skills do you have?
_____

What skills would you like to develop?
_____

What would you like to change right now at work?
_____

Set Goals:

What are your long-term goals?
1 Year: _____
3 Years: _____
5 Years: _____

What are your top 3 short-term goals? What would you like to accomplish in the next 12 months?
1. _____
2. _____
3. _____

Overcome Challenges:

What is the biggest challenge you're facing right now?
_____

Why is this challenge your top priority?
_____

What is this challenge costing you or your organization?
_____

Are there emotional components to this challenge? How does thinking about this challenge make you feel?
_____

What are you willing to do to conquer this challenge?
_____

Once you have conquered this challenge, how will you feel?
_____

Sustain Accountability:

How do you like to be held accountable? Email? Text? Phone calls?
_____

What style of accountability do you like? Gentle suggestions, provocative questions, teachable assignments, deadlines, or directive conversations?
_____

What else is going on in your life that is creating stress or causing you to be distracted?
1. _____
2. _____
3. _____
4. _____

When they discover the center of the universe, a lot of people will be disappointed to discover they are not it.

~BERNARD BAILEY

My top priorities today are:

1. _____

2. _____

3. _____

Today's challenges include:

1. _____

2. _____

3. _____

Leadership skills I need to remember / practice today:

1. _____

2. _____

3. _____

I can encourage others to succeed if I:

1. _____

2. _____

3. _____

Today's accomplishments:

_____
_____
_____

Overall, today was:
- ○ Rough
- ○ Meh
- ○ Okay
- ○ Good
- ○ Great

From today's challenges I learned:

_____
_____

I can make tomorrow even better if I:

_____

5-MINUTE LEADING REMOTE WORKERS PLAN

We all thought we wanted to spend more time at home, and that dream is now a reality.

As leaders, we need to remember that every person's working from home experience is unique. Some employees may have grown children suddenly furloughed from a job, or on permanent spring break from college. Some workers may have young children who need lots of supervision and homeschooling assistance. Parents are learning that it is far more difficult to homeschool a first grader than an eighth grader. There are more families living closer together, which can mean making adjustments. At the same time, they are competing for computer time, bandwidth, and space.

Remote work can be convenient and immensely productive. Many workers find that working from home saves them hours getting ready for work, commuting back and forth, and chatting with co-workers. Remote workers save money on gas, parking, tolls, lunches and coffees, and clothes for work.

Remote work can be wildly efficient when workers are intrinsically motivated, skilled in their jobs, and rewarded for results.

Remote workers also need the right leadership to be effective.

Leaders with remote teams need to:

1. Be flexible.
Strict working hours and punching the clock are not as important as producing the right outcomes.

Leaders need to ask:
Where does my team need flexibility?
_____
_____

What kinds of communication do my people need from me?
_____
_____

How often do I want updates on projects?
_____
_____

How do I want my teams to communicate with me and each other?
_____
_____

2. When people are physically separated they need habits and routine to increase communication.

People are not sitting in their organization's office for leaders to ask questions, or for workers to ask questions of their supervisors, so it is important to plan opportunities to talk with each other.

My team can check in with each other at _____ every _____.

We hold meetings at _____ and we use _____ (link, platform, technology).

3. Make sure employees have the right equipment.
While some organizations and companies issue computers and phones, others do not. Making sure all of your team members have the right equipment with updated software, including cyber security precautions and the right VPN, means they are protecting company information and not using their child's school's iPad to run reports and store budget data.

- *How often are backups run?* _____
- *What level of bandwidth is expected?* _____
- *Where is information stored?* _____
- *What kind of shared systems do we use?* _____
- *What kind of security are we using to prevent viruses and breaches?* _____

If you can lay your head on your pillow each night knowing you gave hundred per cent to your day, success will find you.

~RUSSELL L. MASON

My top priorities today are:

1. _____
2. _____
3. _____

Today's challenges include:

1. _____
2. _____
3. _____

Leadership skills I need to remember / practice today:

1. _____
2. _____
3. _____

I can encourage others to succeed if I:

1. _____
2. _____
3. _____

Today's accomplishments:

_____
_____
_____

Overall, today was:
- ○ Rough
- ○ Meh
- ○ Okay
- ○ Good
- ○ Great

From today's challenges I learned:

_____
_____

I can make tomorrow even better if I:

_____

5-MINUTE
WORK-LIFE BALANCE ASSESSMENT PLAN

On a scale of 1-10, with 1 being very low and 10 being very high, please answer these questions.

_____ How satisfied are you with your life right now?
_____ How happy are you, overall, with your current job?
_____ How happy are you with your current leadership at work?
_____ How important is the work you do?
_____ Do you have the right amount of autonomy in your life?
_____ How satisfied are you with your home life?
_____ If you gave yourself a score for how awesome you are, what would it be?

What are your top work priorities?

1. _____
2. _____
3. _____

What are your top home priorities?

1. _____
2. _____
3. _____

Which of these would make you happier?

○	**More purpose**	work	myself	home
○	**More simplicity**	work	myself	home
○	**More freedom**	work	myself	home
○	**More ambition**	work	myself	home
○	**More achievement**	work	myself	home
○	**More control**	work	myself	home
○	**More healthy habits**	work	myself	home

What would you like to change about your work?

1. _____
2. _____
3. _____

What would make your home life better?

1. _____
2. _____
3. _____

Didn't have a dime, but I always had a vision. Always had high, high, hopes.
~ PANIC AT THE DISCO

My top priorities today are:

1. _____
2. _____
3. _____

Today's challenges include:

1. _____
2. _____
3. _____

Leadership skills I need to remember / practice today:

1. _____
2. _____
3. _____

I can encourage others to succeed if I:

1. _____
2. _____
3. _____

Today's accomplishments:

_____
_____
_____

Overall, today was:
○ Rough
○ Meh
○ Okay
○ Good
○ Great

From today's challenges I learned:

_____
_____

I can make tomorrow even better if I:

_____

5-MINUTE WORKING FROM HOME QUIZ

Congratulations!

We are all finally working from home! No commute. Work in shorts and sweatshirts. Make your own coffee. Take breaks whenever you want. Set your own schedule! Don't worry about people breathing down your neck or looking over your shoulder. The dogs are thrilled to have you home!

Working from home sounds like a great idea, until it is not. Some people thrive when working from home, while others struggle. Knowing what works best for you can be helpful to maximizing your productivity, decreasing your frustration, and staying on track.

We all have a working-from-home personality. Take this short quiz to see what you need to do to maximize your time and resources when working from home. Rate yourself on a scale 1 through 5, with one being not at all true and five being very true.

Not at all true		Meh		Very true
1	2	3	4	5

_____ I am easily frustrated by tasks I do not want to do.

_____ It takes me a long time to warm up to working first thing in the morning.

_____ I am easily distracted by chores and domestic obligations while at home.

_____ I don't like making a daily to-do list.

_____ I like being able to work from any part of the house I want.

_____ I miss working with and being around other people.

_____ I like getting regular positive feedback about the work I do.

_____ I look forward to video conferencing and video chats.

_____ I feel as though I am more distracted when working from home.

_____ I would rather spend the day with my co-workers than my dogs or cats.

Add up all of your numbers.

If your score is between 35-50:

It might be difficult for you to work remotely. You can be easily distracted. You may find it easy to procrastinate on projects you don't like or don't want to do. You may need the structure of an office to be as productive as you can be. While you don't necessarily like a schedule, you do like positive encouragement and reinforcement from other people. You are both energized and held accountable by being around other people. You naturally gravitate toward other people and people respond well to your friendly personality. They miss being around you too.

For you to be most efficient, effective, and productive while working at home, consider these ideas:
1. Set specific times to start working. If you are the manager, it may help you to have an 8 o'clock meeting every day with your team to help you stay focused.
2. Schedule your workday and let your family and friends know that those are working hours, and that you need their help so that you can get work done. You would benefit from a virtual Pomodoro session to help you stay accountable.
3. To help get focused in the morning, talk through your daily schedule and set an hour by hour agenda every day.
4. Your best ideas happen when other people are sharing their ideas and thoughts as well. Use brainstorming apps in order to capture ideas and make sure you don't lose the details.

If your score is between 20-34:

You have discovered that some projects are getting a lot more attention because you're not distracted by all of the other people in your office. You tend to manage several different projects, and all of them want your attention. You perform best with some structure, so that you meet deadlines and don't disappoint other team members. While you like the flexibility of working from home, there are aspects to the office that you miss, especially being around other people's ideas. You schedule routine video conferences to stay on track. Your co-workers describe you as kind, hard-working, and reliable.

You can make the most of this time working from home by:
1. Set up your office so that you start every day organized. Otherwise, it is easy to procrastinate on some of the jobs you don't enjoy.
2. Schedule regular meetings with your leadership and your teams to keep them on track. You are reliable and you expect others to meet deadlines as well.
3. To stay focused, consider outsourcing some of the tasks that can be outsourced. You're highly motivated by getting things crossed off your to-do list.
4. You enjoy getting great ideas from brainstorming sessions with a few other people. Consider using apps that allow you to virtually brainstorm and capture those ideas.

If your score is between 10-19:

You were made to work independently. Remote work is awesome. You are creative and you can focus from practically anywhere. You are self-motivated and you love to work. You have a high degree of work discipline, and you think like an owner. You love that you don't have to waste time with small talk, stupid meetings, or anything else that gets in the way of your focused positivity. It is easy for you to get engrossed in your work, and as a result, you may struggle with maintaining a work-life balance. You are a conscientious worker, and you derive a high degree of satisfaction from accomplishing tasks and goals. You have to guard against getting burned out. You will be one of those workers who do not relish the idea of returning to the office.

You can make the most of this time working from home by:
1. Set specific times to stop working. Resolve to turn off notifications and the computer at a certain time so that you can disconnect.
2. Schedule breaks, walks, and times to work out and eat.
3. Create efficiencies by scheduling meetings with others to make sure you are on the right track. It is easy to assume you are doing things right when you don't get feedback.
4. You trust your ideas, but you still need feedback. Schedule times to talk through your ideas with others to make sure your conclusions and actions are correct.

If you want to improve the organization, you have to improve yourself and the organization gets pulled up with you.

~INDRA NOOTI

My top priorities today are:

1. _____
2. _____
3. _____

Today's challenges include:

1. _____
2. _____
3. _____

Leadership skills I need to remember / practice today:

1. _____
2. _____
3. _____

I can encourage others to succeed if I:

1. _____
2. _____
3. _____

Today's accomplishments:

_____
_____
_____

Overall, today was:
- ○ Rough
- ○ Meh
- ○ Okay
- ○ Good
- ○ Great

From today's challenges I learned:

_____
_____

I can make tomorrow even better if I:

_____

5-MINUTE OPTIMISM PLAN

It can be difficult for even the most positive and optimistic person to stay that way during tough times. Human beings are hardwired to try to be optimistic, but continuous stress and uncertainty can cause people to feel more pessimistic. Optimists are likely to view negative situations as temporary, and they believe they can affect the outcomes. How can we help our people remain optimistic, even during tough times?

People who are optimistic report better health, better productivity, and happier lives. Pessimists tend to experience illness, fatigue, and depression more often than optimists.

Optimism is not being blind to difficulties. Optimism is not being overly naïve. Optimists look for meaning in adversity, which makes them more resilient.

Many psychologists clinically describe "dispositional optimism" as expecting the best possible outcome for any given situation. That definition may be naïve. Optimists CREATE the best possible outcomes from tough situations.

It can be helpful to take a few minutes and work through these categories to help stay positive and optimistic.

Adapting to change.

Changes can be difficult. What recent change have you experienced? Examples might include having a baby, changing jobs, new responsibilities, or working from home.

My biggest change in the past year was
_____

What are three POSITIVE outcomes from this change?
1. _____
2. _____
3. _____

New habits.

It takes weeks to establish new routines. What new habits and routines have you developed lately?

One new habit I have adopted is that now I
_____

What are three POSITIVE outcomes from this change?
1. _____
2. _____
3. _____

Professional changes.

How has your professional life shifted in the past year?
_____

What are three POSITIVE outcomes from this change?
1. _____
2. _____
3. _____

Personal changes.

How has your personal life shifted in the past year?
_____

What are three POSITIVE outcomes from this change?
1. _____
2. _____
3. _____

"It is not our abilities that show us who we really are. It is our choices."
—PROFESSOR DUMBLEDORE

Better to do something imperfectly than to do nothing perfectly.
~ROBERT SCHULLER

My top priorities today are:

1. _____
_____

2. _____
_____

3. _____
_____

Today's challenges include:

1. _____
_____

2. _____
_____

3. _____
_____

Leadership skills I need to remember / practice today:

1. _____
_____

2. _____
_____

3. _____
_____

I can encourage others to succeed if I:

1. _____
_____

2. _____
_____

3. _____
_____

Today's accomplishments:

_____
_____
_____

Overall, today was:
- ○ Rough
- ○ Meh
- ○ Okay
- ○ Good
- ○ Great

From today's challenges I learned:

_____
_____

I can make tomorrow even better if I:

_____

5-MINUTE RESILIENCE PLAN

Resilience is the ability to overcome obstacles, recover quickly, and move forward in the right direction at the right time. Why do some people seem to bounce back from difficulties, setbacks and tragedies, while other people struggle? Is resiliency something that can be taught or is it built in? How can we as leaders help our people be more resilient when dealing with difficulty, change, and crisis?

Some of the toughest people in the world reinforce resiliency through training. How do we adopt some of that training into our day-to-day lives?

1. Keep the right attitude.
People who are unrealistically optimistic may not be considering all issues. People who are constantly pessimistic sometimes live out their own self-fulfilling prophecies. When professional athletes compete, they have to believe that they are competing to win or they will lose. But they also consider both the strengths and weaknesses of their opponents.

Resilient people are both optimistic and realistic.

On the optimism scale of 1 to 5, where am I?_____

1	2	3	4	5
Not optimistic		Average		Very optimistic

On the realism scale of 1 to 5, where am I? _____

1	2	3	4	5
Not realistic		Average		Very realistic

On the optimism scale of 1 to 5, where are my team members? _____

1	2	3	4	5
Not optimistic		Average		Very optimistic

On the realism scale of 1 to 5, where are my team members? _____

1	2	3	4	5
Not realistic		Average		Very realistic

2. Create a plan of action for the next steps.
Many people become mired in negativity and inactivity because they cannot figure out how to get themselves out of the current situation and into the next phase. Having a plan of action for what needs to happen next helps us move forward.

Plan of action:
- Create a worst-case scenario. Create a best-case scenario. The reality is probably somewhere in between.
- Create a list of action steps to take in both situations.
- Prioritize those action steps.
- Break down the action steps into manageable chunks to cross off your list.

3. Develop a timeline.
It is important to maintain a sense of urgency or action steps don't happen. Create a timeline that holds people accountable for their most important action items.

4. Be accountable to yourself and to others.
In interviewing Colonel Lee Ellis, US Air Force (retired), and former prisoner of war in Vietnam, I asked how he was able to maintain honor under some of history's most horrific conditions. He said he felt a sense of accountability to his fellow POWs and he did not want to dishonor them.

I can be accountable to myself by:
_____

I can be accountable to others when I:
_____

I can hold others accountable by:
_____

Don't follow the crowd, let the crowd follow you.
~ MARGARET THATCHER

My top priorities today are:

1. _____
2. _____
3. _____

Today's challenges include:

1. _____
2. _____
3. _____

Leadership skills I need to remember / practice today:

1. _____
2. _____
3. _____

I can encourage others to succeed if I:

1. _____
2. _____
3. _____

Today's accomplishments:

_____
_____
_____

Overall, today was:
○ Rough
○ Meh
○ Okay
○ Good
○ Great

From today's challenges I learned:
_____
_____

I can make tomorrow even better if I:
_____

5-MINUTE STRATEGIC THINKING PLAN

Strategic thinking is about thinking big thoughts, looking toward the needs and products in the future, and crafting the plans needed to move forward. How can we help our teams think bigger? How do we think bigger?

1. See the big picture.
Know as much as possible about your organization and its people. Know what you do and whom you do it for.

We make/produce/provide _____ for _____.

2. Connect the dots.
Great strategic thinkers connect people, ideas, and possibilities, and this requires time to think. Some people think best with another person or people, while others need solitude. Either way, it requires time devoted to thinking.

I best think deeply when I _____
_____.

I brainstorm best with people who _____
_____.

3. Strategic thinkers
Strategic thinkers can tap into both divergent (big picture) and convergent (arranging the puzzle pieces) thinking, and they easily move between them to develop these thinking skills. Try brainstorming with one other person at a time, and try to view the issue from multiple perspectives.

I can brainstorm with _____ to gather information.

I can brainstorm with _____ to gauge how this issue is perceived.

I can brainstorm with _____ to figure out implementation.

I can brainstorm with _____ to see the issue from the outside.

4. Change your environment.
There is a reason many organizations hold "offsites." People need a different place, different stimuli, and to be "pleasantly uncomfortable" to shift thinking. People also need to eliminate distractions.

I can go to _____ to think better.

My team could spend a day at _____ to think.

5. Some leaders hear about strategic thinking initiatives and they dismiss them as being frivolous.
Strategic thinking is about the future of the business and achieving long-term success.

If there were no resource constraints, this company could _____.

If there was unlimited money, we could develop/produce/incorporate/research/solve _____
_____.

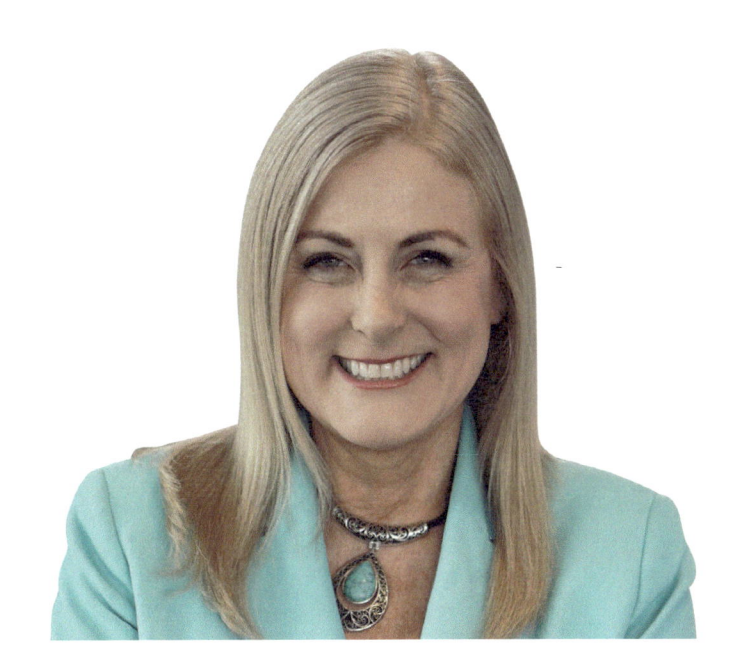

Mary C. Kelly | Ph.D., Commander, U.S. Navy (ret)
CEO, Productive Leaders

Mary specializes in leadership growth that helps organizations improve their profitability and productivity, especially in finance, insurance, real estate, and manufacturing. One of the first female graduates of the Naval Academy, Mary served 25 years on active duty, mostly in Asia, leading multi-cultural teams in nine countries. Her remarkable career of service included working as an intelligence officer, a chief of police, an HR director, and a chief of staff, as well as training more than 40,000 military personnel.

Mary has been a leadership and economics professor at the Naval Academy, the Air Force Academy, and Hawaii Pacific University. She has written 13 business books, including her best-seller, **Master Your World** (named a "must read" by MENSA and MOAA), and her latest award-winner, **Why Leaders Fail and the 7 Prescriptions for Success** (profiled in Forbes and Success magazines).

Today, Mary is a popular conference keynote speaker and leadership adviser working with businesses, associations, and government agencies. She offers programs that are content rich, highly entertaining, and strategically designed to help her clients get results.

www.ProductiveLeaders.com
Mary@ProductiveLeaders.com
Office: (719) 357-7360
Mobile: (443) 995-8663

Follow Mary:

Other Books Available by Mary Include:

The Five Minute Leadership Guide
https://productiveleaders.com/product/the-five-minute-leadership-guide/

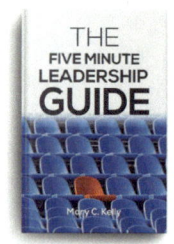

Who Comes Next? Leadership Succession Planning Made Easy
https://productiveleaders.com/product/who-comes-next-leadership-succession-planning-made-easy/

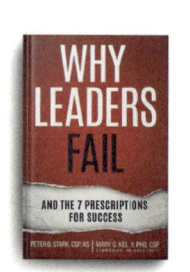

Why Leaders Fail and the 7 Prescriptions for Success
https://productiveleaders.com/product/why-leaders-fail-7-prescriptions-success/

15 Ways to Grow Your Business in Every Economy
https://productiveleaders.com/product/15-ways-to-grow-your-business-in-every-economy/

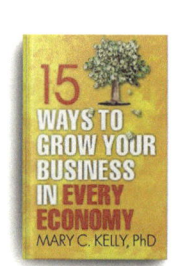

Master Your World
https://productiveleaders.com/product/master-your-world/

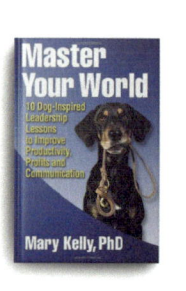

Stop the Barking at Work
https://productiveleaders.com/product/stop-the-barking-at-work/

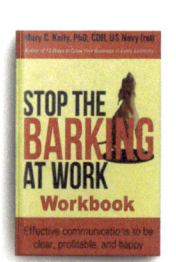

360° of Leadership
https://productiveleaders.com/product/360-of-leadership/

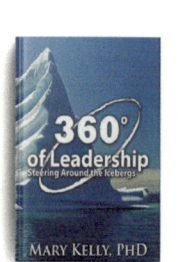

In Case of Emergency Break Glass!
https://productiveleaders.com/product/in-case-of-emergency-break-glass/

Money Smart
https://productiveleaders.com/product/money-smart/

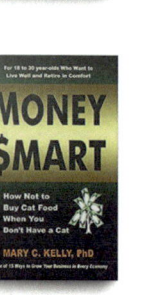